MATTING
AND
FRAMING
MADE
EASY

**STEP-BY-STEP, EASY-TO-MASTER
TECHNIQUES FOR
THE BEGINNING FRAMER**

JANEAN THOMPSON

WATSON-GUPTILL PUBLICATIONS/NEW YORK

HALF-TITLE PAGE:
Untitled. *Ann Hartley. Mixed aqua media on handmade embossed paper. This float-mounted, three-dimensional work has a crisp, professional look. The glass was elevated above the artwork without matting.*

TITLE-PAGE:
Untitled. *Lois Blackburn. Watercolor collage. The subtle matting and framing choices echo the soft, elegant feel of this piece.*

DEDICATION/ACKNOWLEDGMENTS PAGE:
"Hurricane." *Carol Farmayan. Oil on canvas. The natural oak finish of the frame somehow holds the fierceness and activity of this work, the first in a triptych, in place.*

CONTENTS PAGE:
Untitled. *Ann Hartley. Mixed aqua media. The stark, wide, white borders of rag matting give this piece of art a surge of energy. This is a great example of artworks matted and framed for competition, for which white mats are frequently mandatory.*

Senior Editor: Candace Raney
Editor: Liz Harvey
Designer: Areta Buk
Production Manager: Hector Campbell

Copyright © 1996 by Janean Thompson
First published 1996 in the United States by Watson-Guptill Publications,
a division of BPI Communications,
1515 Broadway, New York, NY 10036

Library of Congress Cataloging in Publication Data

Thompson, Janean.
    Matting and framing made easy : step-by-step, easy-to-master
  techniques for the beginning framer / [Janean Thompson].
       p.   cm.
    Includes index.
    ISBN 0-8230-3047-4
    1. Picture frames and framing.   I. Title.
  N8550.T42   1996
  749'.7·—dc20   96-13560
                                             CIP

Manufactured in Malaysia

1 2 3 4 5 6 7 8 9 / 04 03 02 01 00 99 98 97 96

ACKNOWLEDGMENTS

There are many people without whom this book could not have been written. To all of those who helped with your encouragement and excitement, I say, "Thank you!" A special thanks to Candace Raney, Senior Acquisitions Editor, Watson-Guptill Publications, for initiating this project. To Gretchen Curnes, who has believed in me (and told me so, repeatedly) for more than 15 years. To Molly Webb and Cindy Henderson, for always being there.

But gigantic, special thanks to my husband, Bill, for understanding and supporting me throughout the completion of this book.

CONTENTS

CHAPTER 1

GETTING STARTED

An interest in the presentation of your original artworks or your artwork collection might be one of the best reasons to consider framing the pieces yourself. Some of you might regard the economical aspect of this decision to be a strong motivating factor. But the satisfaction of framing one of your original artworks from start to finish might be the most important reason for doing your own framing. You can be in complete charge of the way a piece will look when completed without relying on anyone else to do the presentation for you. All the colors, textures, and special decorative touches are up to you.

You need only a few basic pieces of equipment to complete a framing project.

A PROFESSIONAL LOOK

You can present inexpensive posters in such a way to make them resemble fine art. Here, a double mat, nonglare glass, and a color-coordinated metal frame combine to give a photography poster a dressy look.

I can't overemphasize the value of proper, professional-quality presentation. Adequate framing always appears to be just that. By employing some of the presentation ideas covered here, you can transform your framed works from ordinary to above average. Changes as basic as using wider mat borders, for example, can make a project look more elegant than it otherwise would. Similarly, a better match of frame style and artwork style can improve the presentation of the piece. Learn ways to give your artwork the special qualities of strength and unified enhancement. Anyone can accomplish this polished, above-average look with little struggle.

My purpose here is to provide those of you who have hesitated, for whatever reason, with the assurance to get started. For those who have already done framing, you'll learn additional information that can make the process easier, as well as give your finished project an individual, unique appearance. The in-depth procedures that follow give you many options that could improve the presentation of your originals or your collection.

So, get ready to read and to apply the simple, exciting, and rewarding guidelines and ideas that can transform any artwork into a cohesive, elegant package. I include everything you need to know in easy-to-follow steps, which are accompanied by pictures. These techniques cover equipment essentials, work-space setups, measuring and mounting approaches, matting choices, cutting methods, and framing tips.

SETTING UP

You can begin framing your artwork collection without purchasing any expensive equipment. Chances are you already have everything you need to complete a basic frame project. Special tools make the job a bit easier, but all you actually need to put an artwork "sandwich" into a frame is a hammer to tap a few long, thin nails into place. By purchasing ready-made frames and having glass cut to size, you might only have to cut a piece of backing to size using a ruler and a utility knife. Only when your framing becomes more customized will you potentially have to buy a few items to speed up your results. Such tools as miter boxes, saws, brad pushers, and glass cutters might be helpful at this point.

Finding a place to work is easy, too. A kitchen often has the best lighting in a home, and the table usually provides a large enough surface for you to work on. But keep in mind that using the kitchen table poses some problems. The table is frequently in demand, so you'll be forced to set up and break down every time you want to do a framing project. Also, the average height of a kitchen table is a bit low for most people. And over the lifespan of a project, this working position becomes uncomfortable. A table that is 33 to 35 inches high is ideal; you won't have to bend over as low, so less back strain occurs. This is especially important if you're going to be working on several projects in succession. To start, though, the kitchen table or the dining-room table (if you have one) is fine.

As the number and size of your projects grow, so will your need for more space in a segregated area. When you reach this point, the most likely spot for you to set up shop in is the garage or basement. With the cabinets, tables, shelves, and bins ordinarily located in these areas, they make wonderful work spaces. In addition, you can design a worktable to serve your individual requirements.

When you first get involved with framing projects, setting up a dining-room workshop is a viable option. This sample layout efficiently uses a 10 × 12-foot room. There is ample storage space for materials beneath the 4 × 4-foot worktable, and the file cabinet and shelves accommodate paperwork and projects in various stages of completion, respectively.

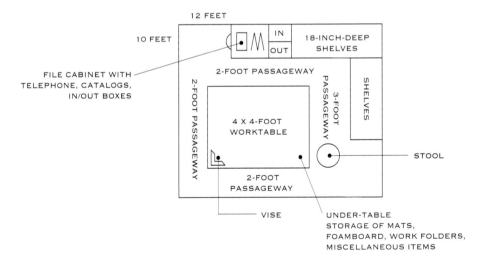

In time, you might find that the number of framing projects you're doing calls for you to switch from a makeshift setup in your house to a single-garage workshop. This layout shows how to successfully fit an at-home business in a 10 × 20-foot area. This garage offers large areas for project work, materials storage, filing, and other paperwork.

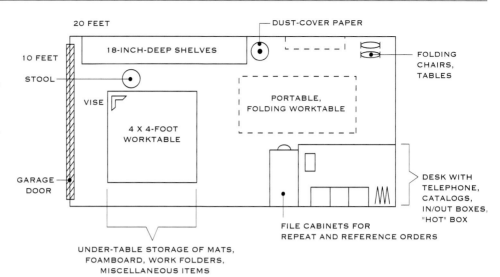

20 FEET

18-INCH-DEEP SHELVES

DUST-COVER PAPER

FOLDING CHAIRS, TABLES

10 FEET

STOOL

VISE

4 X 4-FOOT WORKTABLE

PORTABLE, FOLDING WORKTABLE

GARAGE DOOR

DESK WITH TELEPHONE, CATALOGS, IN/OUT BOXES, "HOT" BOX

FILE CABINETS FOR REPEAT AND REFERENCE ORDERS

UNDER-TABLE STORAGE OF MATS, FOAMBOARD, WORK FOLDERS, MISCELLANEOUS ITEMS

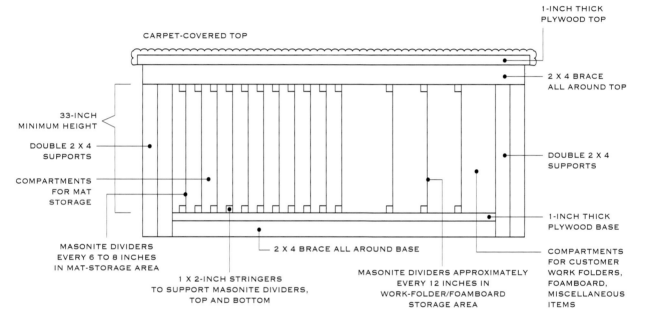

CARPET-COVERED TOP

1-INCH THICK PLYWOOD TOP

2 X 4 BRACE ALL AROUND TOP

33-INCH MINIMUM HEIGHT

DOUBLE 2 X 4 SUPPORTS

COMPARTMENTS FOR MAT STORAGE

DOUBLE 2 X 4 SUPPORTS

1-INCH THICK PLYWOOD BASE

2 X 4 BRACE ALL AROUND BASE

COMPARTMENTS FOR CUSTOMER WORK FOLDERS, FOAMBOARD, MISCELLANEOUS ITEMS

MASONITE DIVIDERS EVERY 6 TO 8 INCHES IN MAT-STORAGE AREA

1 X 2-INCH STRINGERS TO SUPPORT MASONITE DIVIDERS, TOP AND BOTTOM

MASONITE DIVIDERS APPROXIMATELY EVERY 12 INCHES IN WORK-FOLDER/FOAMBOARD STORAGE AREA

Above: In addition to dimensions, this side view of a suitable worktable shows the various compartments for storing such materials as mats, work folders, and foamboard. Covering the top of the worktable with a firm, low-nap carpet remnant provides cushioning for the frame finish and prevents mat scarring.

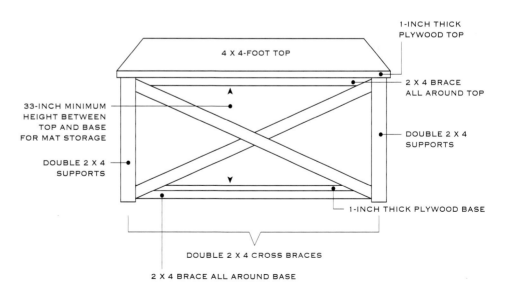

4 X 4-FOOT TOP

1-INCH THICK PLYWOOD TOP

2 X 4 BRACE ALL AROUND TOP

33-INCH MINIMUM HEIGHT BETWEEN TOP AND BASE FOR MAT STORAGE

DOUBLE 2 X 4 SUPPORTS

DOUBLE 2 X 4 SUPPORTS

1-INCH THICK PLYWOOD BASE

DOUBLE 2 X 4 CROSS BRACES

2 X 4 BRACE ALL AROUND BASE

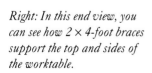

Right: In this end view, you can see how 2 × 4-foot braces support the top and sides of the worktable.

CHAPTER 2

MEASURING

Before you can do anything in preparation for framing your artwork, you must complete an essential step: properly measuring the image you want to display. Every other part of the process is based on this critical measurement. To this image size, you add the dimensions of all the borders in order to determine the final frame size. Whether you eventually order a custom frame, buy a ready-made frame, decide to mount the artwork, or use a mat to enhance the piece, the size and shape of the image you'll exhibit in that frame is the first set of figures you need.

With any accurate measuring device, you can determine the measurements needed to plan and complete a framing project.

DETERMINING IMAGE SIZE

Before you can measure the size of image, you must define what this is. Image size refers to the actual picture area, excluding any border. The picture area is the part of the artwork that you want to display within the window of a mat.

Careful measurement is important and, fortunately, easy. The only tool you need to determine image size with precision is a ruler or measuring tape. Use a pencil and pad to record the figures. Always use pencil to make any calculations. If you make an accidental pencil mark on an artwork, you have some chance of removing it. Pen ink, on the other hand, can destroy a valuable piece of art in a flash. Also, be gentle when you lay a ruler or tape measure against an artwork's surface. Some surfaces are easily scratched and ruined. After you double-check that you've read the measuring device correctly, you can proceed. Remember, measure twice, and cut once.

You can calculate image size via two basic methods. One approach requires two measuring steps. First, figure out the exact size of the picture area by measuring its length and width. Then from each of these measurements, subtract $1/4$ inch. These numbers represent a $1/8$-inch decrease on each side of the image and enable the mat to overlap the edge of the picture area by that tiny amount. This $1/8$-inch overlap ensures that the border color won't intrude in the image window of the mat. If the image doesn't have a border, the slight overlap will be sufficient to properly hold the artwork behind the mat.

The other approach, which most professional framers prefer, is a bit more direct. It eliminates one of the steps listed above, as well as the possibility of miscalculation. To determine the image area using this method, begin measuring $1/8$ inch inside the border of the picture and end $1/8$ inch before the picture's opposite edge. The result is the exact image area you want to mat, with no subtraction necessary. You can, of course, use whichever method feels better to you and yields consistently correct results. But remember that the accuracy of this first set of figures determines the accuracy of all other measurements.

One way to calculate image size is to measure the exact picture area and then subtract a bit for edge overlap.

Another method for measuring image size is to automatically subtract the edge overlap from the picture area.

DETERMINING IMAGE SIZE

On those occasions when you're working with a piece of art that is signed or signed and numbered, you'll probably want to include those features in the visible image area. The signature and number are usually located on the border of the print or on the mounting material around the original work. This border is a solid light color and obviously not part of the pictorial area. If you measure the image area so that you include only the signature and nothing extra on the top and sides, the image will look out of balance. To improve the appearance of the artwork, you should include all of the signature and a portion of the border on the top and the sides. If the artist's signature is large, include all of it but don't use a white border area around the print that is equal to the signature strip. To achieve harmony and lessen the "competition" between the white strip and the art image, you can use a border area of $1/4$ inch to $5/16$ inch (perhaps $3/8$ inch in rare cases) on the top and sides regardless of the width of the signature area.

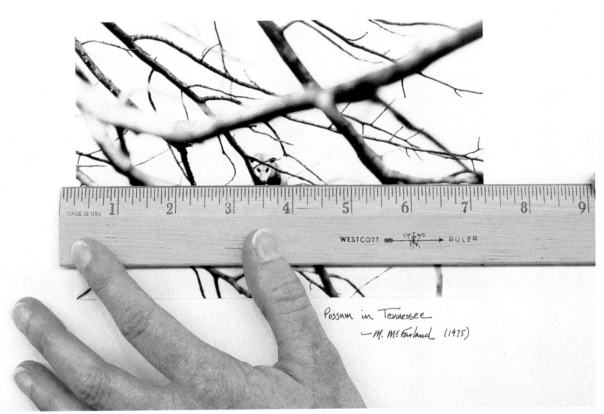

For proper balance, leave some space all around the picture, not just in the signature area.

DETERMINING MAT AND FRAME SIZES

After successfully measuring the image size you want to display, the next simple step is to calculate the size of the frame you should purchase. This involves figuring out the size of the mat borders you want to have visible around the image; consult the width guidelines that follow (see the chart below). Once you determine the mat size, add these measurements in pairs to the image size. Here, one pair represents two sides—either the widths or the lengths—of the mat surrounding the picture. In other words, you add the width choice to each side of the image measurement. For example, an 8 × 10-inch image with a 2-inch mat all around it has a perimeter of 12 × 14 inches. You add 2 inches to each of the four sides of the image.

Frequently, framers have a hard time deciding on the size of the mat border to use with any given size of image. Largely, the choice is an individual one. The mat-width figures listed below are general suggestions; they aren't written in stone. The needs of each piece of art and various decorating requirements will have a bearing on your decisions. Ideally, the widths of the mat borders should complement the artwork, rather than simply accommodate it.

The size of the space in which you plan to place the artwork often dictates the matting width. Sometimes you need to fit an odd-sized piece of art into a ready-made frame. Be careful using narrow borders. They often make the artwork look as if it has been squeezed and forced into a frame even though you may have had various options available to you and decided on small borders.

When you first start determining mat and frame sizes, you may run into some difficulties. Suppose that when you place the artwork behind the finished mat window, you discover that the window is too small and the mat covers too much of the image. Most likely, you failed to add both pairs of mat widths to the image size. Otherwise, you may have miscalculated the image size originally.

IMAGE-SIZE AND MAT-WIDTH GUIDELINES (IN INCHES)

IMAGE SIZE	MAT WIDTH
5 × 7	1 to $1^1/_2$
8 × 10	$1^1/_2$ to 2
11 × 14	2 to $2^1/_2$
16 × 20	$2^1/_2$ to 3
20 × 24	3 to $3^1/_2$
24 × 30	$3^1/_2$ to 4

DETERMINING MAT AND FRAME SIZES

Another potential problem is having a tiny bit of the border around the print show when you position the artwork behind the mat window. Remember, the image size and the mat opening are very close to the same measurement. In this situation, you probably forgot to subtract the overlap from the image area.

You might also encounter the problem of the print falling through the window. This happens when you don't take into consideration all-around overlapping. Be sure to allow for $\frac{1}{8}$-inch minimum coverage around the edges. After you calculate the border-width total, add this number to the image-area measurement. The resulting figures indicate the size of the frame needed for this particular artwork.

Mat borders that are too narrow make the artwork seem haphazardly squeezed into the frame rather than planned.

FRAMING ODD-SIZED ARTWORK

Placing an irregular-sized piece of art into a ready-made frame is, quite frankly, one of the most difficult calculating challenges you'll face. Because the proportions aren't exact, you must pay special attention to your mathematical calculations. Suppose, for example, that you're working with an 8×10-inch vertical photograph. When you take into account edge overlap, the image size is reduced to $7^3/_4 \times 9^3/_4$ inches. The frame size is 11×14 inches.

After you establish the image width and length (remembering to leave a bit of the image for overlap), subtract those numbers from the frame width and length, respectively. The remainders constitute the borders around the image area. In this example, $11 - 7^3/_4 = 3^1/_4$ (border width), and $14 - 9^3/_4 = 4^1/_4$ (border length). You can position the image within those measurements two ways.

Using one method, you first divide the width difference by 2 (see the chart below). The figure you come up with is the dimension of each mat border on the left and right sides of the image. Next, divide the length difference by 2. This figure is the dimension of each mat border above and below the image.

METHOD 1: CORRESPONDING IMAGE, BORDER, AND FRAME SIZES

	WIDTH (IN INCHES)	LENGTH (IN INCHES)
IMAGE SIZE	8	10
	$-^1/_4$	$-^1/_4$
	$7^3/_4$	$9^3/_4$
FRAME SIZE	11	14

Difference
$11 - 7^3/_4 = 3^1/_4$ $14 - 9^3/_4 = 4^1/_4$
Differences Divided by 2 to Determine Borders
$3^1/_4 \div 2 = 1^5/_8$ $4^1/_4 \div 2 = 2^1/_8$

Using the second method, you first divide the width difference by 2 (see the chart below). This figure represents the size of the mat borders above and on the sides of the image. Next, subtract this figure from the length difference. The remainder constitutes the dimension of the mat border below the image.

METHOD 2: CORRESPONDING IMAGE, BORDER, AND FRAME SIZES

	WIDTH (IN INCHES)	LENGTH (IN INCHES)
IMAGE SIZE	8	10
	$-^1/_4$	$-^1/_4$
	$7^3/_4$	$9^3/_4$
FRAME SIZE	11	14

Difference
$11 - 7^3/_4 = 3^1/_4$ $14 - 9^3/_4 = 4^1/_4$
Difference Divided by 2 to Determine Top and Side Borders
$3^1/_4 \div 2 = 1^5/_8$
Length Difference Minus Top-Border Size to Determine Bottom Border
$4^1/_4 - 1^5/_8 = 2^5/_8$

FRAMING ODD-SIZED ARTWORK

When the proportions of a piece of art and a frame aren't the same, you need to balance the image and the mat.

An image positioned in a way that produces a heavy bottom can be more pleasing than one with uneven borders between the top and bottom and the sides.

WORKING WITH EXTRA-WIDE BORDERS

Artists who create limited-edition prints, such as intaglio, woodcuts, etchings, and monotypes, often place their images in the center of the paper and leave wide borders all around. They do this for two primary reasons. The proper registration of individually handprinted art is difficult to achieve. Providing a wide border allows for some margin of error in image placement, as well as slight shifts in the placement. The other common reason is that the artists think that wide margins complement their images and consider them part of the desired look of the work.

As you begin measuring, keep in mind that any alteration of the piece of art results in an immediate depreciation in the artwork's value. When you trim excess border paper from a print, you alter the finished work from the way its creator originally presented it. This change destroys the expected escalation in value of the artwork.

So mat the image with whatever mat width needed to cover the paper on which the print was made. This may result in an unusual look or one that resembles a museum presentation, but it most likely is the way the artist envisioned the framed work. Cutting the paper size will destroy the resale value of the artwork, which is especially important if the artist becomes prominent. In the end, however, the choice to reduce the paper size and use small mat widths is yours.

"Barn Owl" is a great example of an artist signing a work along the lower edge of the paper that a handcolored etching was placed on. In order for the signature and title to be visible, the mat window was cut to expose large borders on the print. Artwork courtesy of Nicholas Vinall.

CHAPTER 3

MOUNTING

Mounting has been a part of artwork presentation for decades. The purpose of mounting is to secure the piece of art in place in some fashion, with or without a mat, so that you display it in a frame for viewing. Mounting isn't the jazzy, showy part of framing. In fact, people seldom, if ever, see it. It doesn't offer the fun and excitement of presentation that matting, with its variety of colors, textures, and fancy cuts, does. But, being familiar with different mounting methods and knowing how they'll affect artwork as well as how long they'll last are important parts of the mounting process. Framers have many options. You can choose from among several conservation techniques; some are fast and simple artwork-friendly mounting methods, and some are permanent mounting methods. None of these techniques calls for specialized and/or expensive equipment. In fact, the required materials are available at most framing- and art-supply centers.

Acid-free mounting materials are available in many forms. Although not all are conservation quality, each is ideally suited for a specific application.

ARCHIVAL MOUNTING

In archival, or conservation, mounting, everything that touches the artwork is acid-free. In fact, the materials are 100 percent rag content. This means that unlike regular mat board and backing supplies, which are composed of wood pulp, archival materials are made up of all-cotton fibers. In conservation mounting, you isolate the artwork within a capsule of protection.

When you are ready to do archival mounting, you'll discover that the materials you need are surprisingly easy to gather. Rag matting, rag backing, mounting corners, mounting strips, acid-free liquid adhesives, acid-free tapes, and rice and wheat starches are available at most art-supply stores. You can also find them at catalog-order facilities that sell framing materials. Archival-mounting materials should be on every framer's shelf. These are the best products you can use in your fine-art presentations. Their cost is quite low in comparison to the value of the protection they provide.

Keep in mind that there is no adequate substitute for many of the acid-free materials designed for specific mounting purposes. You might come across some handmade alternatives for mounting corners, and one adhesive can eliminate the need for several products. However, archival-quality materials are critical to the preservation of your valuable works of art.

Because the entire archival-mounting process is so quick and easy, it may become your favorite way to mount the artwork you frame. After you collect the necessary materials and set up your workspace, cut the backing foamboard to the frame size needed, following the guidelines for measuring. The foamboard must be all rag-covered in order to be considered archival quality. You can either purchase rag-covered foamboard, or place a barrier of rag paper on top of conventional foamboard.

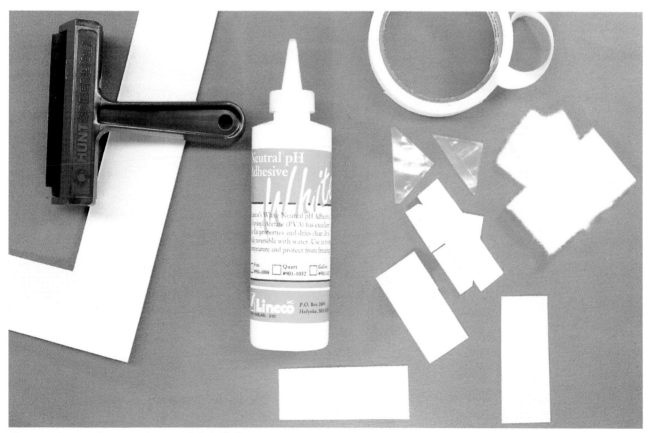

Conservation-quality mounting materials include paper and acetate corner pockets, and acid-free adhesive and tapes.

ARCHIVAL MOUNTING

Measure and cut the outside perimeters of your chosen rag mat or mats. Begin the conservation mounting by cutting the window in the rag mats according to the desired border widths. After you place the acid-free, foamboard backing on your work surface, lay the artwork on top of the rag foamboard, and center the artwork by sight. Next, set the windowed mat over the artwork, and adjust its position. When the print is placed exactly, lay a clean weight in the center, and then lift off the colored border mat. As a clean weight, you can use, for example, a plastic bag (that you've closed securely, of course) filled with dry beans, unpopped popcorn kernels, or marbles, or a smooth-bottomed paperweight.

You can use commercially made or handmade acid-free corner pockets to hold the art piece in place. If you use commercial conservation corners, simply peel one off the paper strip, and slip it over one of the artwork's four corners. Repeat the procedure for the other three corners. Finally, gently press down all four corners to be sure that they're properly adhered.

Instead of buying commercially made corners, you might decide to create your own in order to save money. They are quick and easy to make, and represent another way to economize while giving your artwork the very best handling. Simply cut, fold, and affix corner pockets, which you can make from any all-rag artists' paper. Position and hold the print in place as described earlier. Then slip a handmade pocket over each of the four corners, with the tails under the artwork and the triangular pocket on top of the artwork. The next step is to put a strip of acid-free tape diagonally over the pocket. The tape that extends past the edges of the pocket will secure it, thereby holding the artwork in place. Press firmly to ensure a good bond.

When a piece of art has a small border, the corner pockets may intrude into the image area when they are in place beneath the mat. The solution to this is simple and works for both commercial and handmade pockets. First, visually note the amount of each corner pocket that you can see with the mat in its correct position on top of the print. Notice that each corner pocket may require a different amount of adjustment. After you remove the matting, take the piece of art out of the pockets (you can slip it right back into place once you make the alterations). Set both the mat and the artwork aside in a safe, clean place.

Next, slip a small scrap of matting into one of the pockets that needs trimming. With an X-Acto knife or another sharp cutting device, cut a pie-shaped wedge from the pocket. Repeat on any of the other pockets that have to be made smaller.

Three commonly used thicknesses of foamboard measure (from bottom to top) $1/8$, $1/4$, and $1/2$ inches.

When you begin mounting a piece of art, center it by sight first.

You can use any clean weight to help hold the print in position.

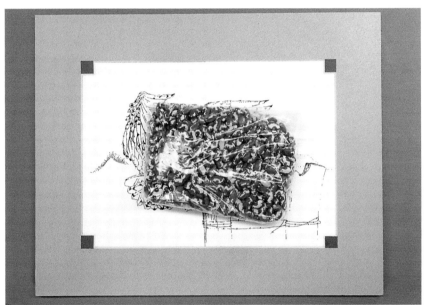

Once you've properly positioned the artwork, attach a commercial corner pocket, and simply press the art into place. You don't need to use tape.

Next, put the artwork back in the pockets. Replace the mat, and check to see that no pocket material shows on any of the four corners. The integrity of the corner pocket isn't lost as long as sufficient pocket edges can hold the print in place. The minimum width acceptable is about ¼ inch.

Ideally, you should use all-rag mats for conservation framing. If for any reason you choose to use a mat that is buffered to be acid-free rather than all-rag, you'll still be able to complete a conservation mounting using that mat. Cut the mat exactly as you would for any other kind of framing. Carefully cut strips of all-rag artists' quality paper (barrier paper) that are slightly narrower than the mat borders. Attach these to the back of the buffered mat with acid-free adhesive. Allow the assembly to dry completely.

Once the mounting materials are dry, place the mat over the image, and continue the framing procedure. The barrier strips, which provide an acceptable degree of protection, fall within the conservation parameters. Check to see that the strips are close enough to the window opening to protect the piece of art beneath it, but not so close that they show.

Your choice of glass or glazing materials is also important when it comes to conservation framing (see page 90). Base your decision on the type of material to select on the requirements of your project. And keep in mind that for a completely archival presentation of a piece of art in a wooden frame, you must seal the rabbet of the frame with a sealer. Applying three coats of an acrylic painting medium, another polymer artists' product, or a water-based wood sealer, is sufficient to restrict the wood sap from migrating into the materials and damaging the artwork.

The beauty of conservation mounting is two-fold. First, you can complete a conservation presentation with ease. Second, your piece of art is provided maximum protection from contamination by damaging materials. The difference in cost is minimal when compared to the end result.

If you offer your artwork for sale, you can use conservation-mounting methods as a selling tool. Clients will appreciate the way you respect your creations. When you show them that you care about how your work is presented, they'll also care. In addition, heirloom pieces of art and photographs have a special need to be handled and presented with care. Conservation mounting is the ideal way to display such items while affording them the best protection from acid migration and impurities.

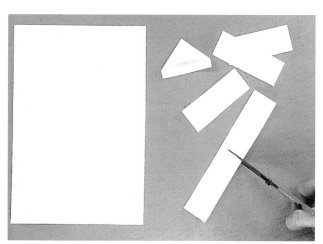

You can make your own corner pockets from acid-free paper strips.

Fold each end of the strip toward the center to create a perfect corner. After you slip the pocket over the corners of the art piece, use acid-free tape to hold it in position.

When mat borders are narrow, the corner pocket might be visible.

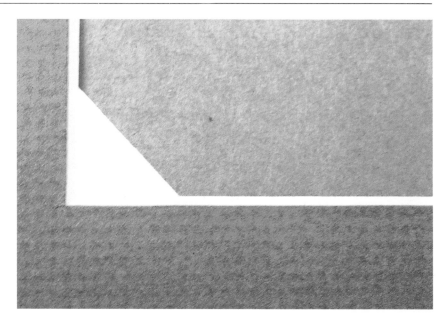

Cut a wedge out of the corner pocket, and replace the mat.

When you cover the back of a regular mat with acid-free paper, you can use it for conservation matting. I chose blue paper for this project because I wanted it to show. White all-rag paper is usually recommended.

SLINGS, FLANGES, AND PROPS

When you frame large pieces of art, you might have to provide additional support along their lower edges. You can do this two ways, neither of which requires adhesive/artwork contact. The first approach involves a type of sling. Here, the sling takes the form of a folded strip of acid-free paper in which the lower edge of the artwork rests. You make the folds in such a way that permits you to apply adhesive to the sling, not to the artwork.

The second method of support calls for flanges. These are commercially made strips of mylar or acetate that are adhesive-backed. The front of the strip extends over the edge of the piece of art, which sits against the base. Because the flange is self-sticking, it doesn't require any additional adhesive.

Another option is to create your own props similar to flanges. Cut a strip of all-rag artists' material of similar thickness to the artwork. The strip should be about 1¹/₂ inches wide and 3 inches long. Slide the prop against the bottom edge of the artwork, and then carefully put a piece of acid-free tape on the prop to hold it in place. Make sure that no tape touches the art. You can use pressure-sensitive, acid-free linen tape, Filmoplast acid-free tape, and artists' acid-free tape.

While slings, flanges, and props are designed to be used in tandem with conservation corners or corner pockets, you can theoretically use them alone. In these situations, you must attach several props or slings along each edge of a piece of art in order to hold it securely. For example, some oversize works of art need two slings. Here, you place the slings along the bottom of the artwork, evenly spaced between the corner pockets. Similarly, you can use flanges along the perimeter of large artworks to hold them in place. Evenly space three or four flanges along each side of the artwork. The overlap on the front of the art and the base along the edge of the art combine to hold the piece in position.

I made this folded sling by hand from all-rag paper.

This piece of art is held in place with acid-free tape and a sling. The tape shouldn't come in contact with the artwork.

Because this flange strip is self-adhesive, all you have to do to attach it is cut and press.

Flanges are similar to slings, but you can also use them alone to support an artwork all around the edges.

Hold the handmade flange in place with acid-free tape.

SINK MOUNTING AND MATTING

To accommodate some pieces of art that are heavy or thick, such as those painted on a thick watercolor paper, an alternative method of support has been developed. Sink mounting and matting involves a basic, straightforward principal. This ingenious approach doesn't call for the use of adhesives of any type, nor does it require attaching a large, heavy artwork via hinges.

In sink mounting, you cover the outside edges of the artwork with a top mat. Measure the image size first, and then add the border widths to determine the frame size. Cut the surround mat to that size. Next, position the artwork on the surround mat, and trace around the artwork. Cut a window in the surround mat into which you'll set the artwork. This surround mat resembles a collar around the work, holds the artwork in place laterally, and provides support for the top mat.

You should cut the surround mat from all-rag material that is the same thickness as the art piece. If the surround mat is too thick, the artwork might appear floppy in the frame. If, on the other hand, the surround mat is too thin, the edges of the mat window will lift and the package will look forced and cramped in the frame. Cut the mat window, and lay it on top of the surround mat. Glue the top decorative mat to the surround mat, and glue the surround mat to the backing. If you anticipate matting or framing the piece a second time at a later date, don't over-glue the mat, backing, and surround mat together. You might damage the art when you attempt replacement. You can also cut slits in the surround mat and backing material, and join them by feeding acid-free tape through the slits.

Rather than cut a surround mat from a fresh piece of matting, you can fill in around the artwork with strips of clean, scrap, all-rag matting. Again, remember to cut the strips from all-rag material that is the same thickness as the artwork. This will ensure a proper support and flush mount for the decorative top mats.

Sink mounting is also useful for any slightly three-dimensional artwork that is too heavy to trust to hinges. The relief of the artwork may require the elevation of the top mat. You can also mount pieces of art with irregular edges using the sink method, but keep in mind that these edges might be an important part of the artwork. If you do sink-mount an odd-shaped work, simply cut the surround mat to the shape of the artwork and then uniformly cover the edges to clean up the presentation.

Begin a sink mount by defining the perimeter of the artwork on the surface of the surround mat.

Cut along the lines to create a window to hold the piece of art.

Test the fit of the surround mat by positioning it around the artwork.

Once the surround mat is in place around the art, you can position the decorative mat on top.

To attach the various components of the project, you can either glue the backing, the surround mat, and the top mat together or cut slits and tape them together.

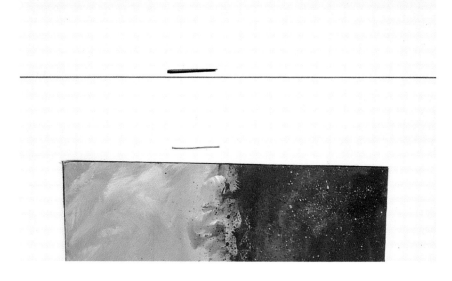

HINGES

One of the most direct ways to mount a piece of art is to attach it with rice-paper hinges. The purpose of the hinges is to hold the art firmly in position with the smallest amount of contact with adhesives possible. For many years, rice-paper hinges and natural rice starch have been used for hinge-making and were the very best way to mount artwork. Museums and conservators continue to use them because they can be removed without harming the artwork.

While rice-paper hinges are considered to be an acid-free mounting technique when acid-free materials are incorporated into them, these hinges physically touch the work. As a result, you must be cautious whenever you attach and remove them. Simply lightly wet the adhesive, let it set for a moment, and then lift off the hinge. Any alteration to the art piece isn't permanent; you can easily remove adhesive residue left after the release of the hinge with a dampened cloth.

You can choose among the two styles of rice-paper hinges used extensively and a couple of special-purpose styles. The two used most of the time are called T hinges and V hinges. T hinges, which are visible above the artwork, are appropriate when the piece of art is attached to a mounting board or mat. The V hinge is invisible behind the artwork. A seldom-used but nevertheless important hinge is the S hinge.

Each hinge is composed of two pieces of torn hinging material (see below). A minimum of two hinges is used to hold any artwork. You can attach any number of hinges when you need to secure a large piece of art. It is smart to consider adding more hinges when the size of the piece dictates that using only two hinges will separate them by 12 to 15 inches. You should also consider the weight of the artwork. Heavy works may require you to space hinges more closely together than light works.

Your goal is to use the minimal amount of adhesive contact that holds that artwork in place. You might need a few chances to get the ratio of hinges, weight, and size to work together. But hinges offer a speedy and accurate way to mount many pieces of art.

Once you attach the hinges, let them dry under pressure. This will ensure not only a tight bond but also a flat appearance. Simply affix the hinges; position the assembly under a smooth surface, such as Plexiglas, glass, or laminate scrap; and

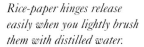

Rice-paper hinges release easily when you lightly brush them with distilled water.

place a weight on top of the assembly. You can use books, bean bags, or bricks, among other objects. Drying the hinges for 24 hours while weighing them down should be sufficient.

When you work with rice-paper hinge material, you should tear rather than cut it. Tearing exposes a soft, fibrous edge that grips firmly. Begin with strips about 1½ inches wide and 3 inches long. Practice will help you alter your needs according to the specific project on hand.

You need rice starch to attach hinges to the backing material. Although many rice-starch manufacturers suggest cooking their product in a double boiler or an egg poacher, I think cooking it in a microwave oven for about 15 to 20 seconds is easiest. Be careful about the quality of the water you use to make the adhesive or to remove a hinge. I highly recommend distilled water, which is free of chemicals. Contaminants found in tap water, such as minerals and metals, can cause the adhesive to discolor with time. This discoloration might be detrimental to the artwork. Mix the paste in small batches; it doesn't contain any preservatives and spoils quickly.

When the milky liquid turns to a clear gel, the paste is ready. Allow it to cool, and then use a clean brush to apply the rice starch in a moderate amount to the hinge material. This ensures a good grip without you're having to remove excess paste. When you work with thin pieces of art, a slight wrinkling might occur as the hinge dries. If this happens, dampen the hinge and dry it under a weight again.

Although attaching hinges is a straightforward process, they sometimes fail. The artwork falls behind the mat, and you must repeat the hinging procedure. Two factors can cause this problem. First, the weight of the rice paper you've chosen may be too light. Try a museum mounting kit, which contains a general-purpose, medium-weight paper that is suitable for most projects. Second, you may not be using enough rice-starch adhesive, so add a bit more the next time.

You might also encounter a problem when you work with thin papers: the hinges show. Unfortunately, this is one of the applications in which hinge use is limited. If hinges show through the paper you're mounting, you'll have to consider using either a different type of mounting or less hinging material within the image area. It is possible to use a short piece of hinging material on the backside of the artwork if it is lightweight.

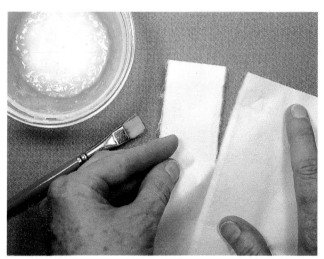

All hinges require two pieces of hinge material. Tear the rice paper to create soft, feathered edges. These edges grip more securely.

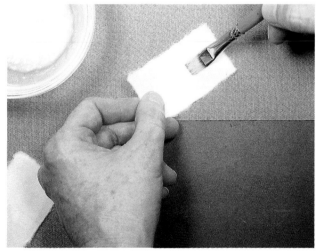

Apply starch-based paste to the hinge parts with a brush. Even, moderate application is suggested.

ARCHIVAL MOUNTING

T HINGES

This hinge style, whose name describes the look of the hinge, is used more than all others. To attach a T hinge, place its base piece on the backside of the artwork, half directly on the art and half above it. You can position the first section of the hinge either horizontally or vertically on the back of the art piece. Next, you lay a cross piece over the section above the artwork, attaching it to the backing material. Each end of the artwork should have its own hinge to guarantee that the work stays perfectly straight behind the mat. Then either trim or fold over any excess hinge material above the cross piece, or add a second reinforcing cross piece.

If you prefer to attach your work to the back of the mat, simply mount the artwork in place behind the mat with two strips of rice paper. Next, put a cross piece over the half of the hinge above the artwork. This cross piece strengthens the hinge without exposing the artwork to additional adhesive.

There is no rule as to whether you should attach the work to the mounting board or to the mat. Some framers consider the look of the mat and artwork to be more unified when the piece of art is attached to the backside of the mat than when it is attached to the mounting board. Other framers, however, prefer to hinge the artwork to the mounting board because they find it easy to hold the piece in place while attaching the hinges. Try both methods, and decide for yourself.

To complete a T hinge, you have to attach half of the hinge to the back of the artwork. Then cross the other half of the hinge, which is above the art, with the second piece of hinge material to form a T.

You should use at least two hinges on all artwork. Large, heavy pieces of art might require more than two hinges.

V HINGES

Because these hinges are invisible beneath the artwork, they are ideal for displaying a piece of art so that it appears to be suspended on the backing surface. Framers usually turn to V hinges when the edges of the piece are important to the artistic statement. People frequently opt for this application when working with an artwork that has textured deckle edges. Here, the background surface becomes a vital part of the look of the finished work. You attach the V hinges to the artwork before you position it on the mat surface. You can then hold the edges of the hinges under the art piece and position them in such a way that prevents them from showing.

To make a V hinge, fold a piece of rice paper and attach half to the back of the artwork. Then slip a coated strip beneath the folded portion of the hinge. Lightly cover all surfaces facing you with starch paste; these are now ready to be put on the background.

Carefully place the artwork onto the colored backing surface. When the artwork is in the proper position, the field becomes a part of the design statement. If you decide to use a top mat, cut the window large enough to show some of the background color. This mounting method creates a feeling of depth and dimension that no other attachment technique offers.

A V hinge is created by folding the first piece of hinge material to form a V. Half of this hinge is attached to the artwork.

A cross piece is placed beneath the loose tail of the hinge, with the adhesive facing outward.

Once you put the adhesive-coated hinges in place, lay the work onto a background color.

ARCHIVAL MOUNTING

FLOATED ARTWORK

You can increase the depth and appeal of a V-hinged art mounting. By elevating the mats around the piece of art, you can give the image an extra degree of importance. If you do this effectively, the image will seem to float. Elevation is easy to accomplish. First, attach strips of scrap foamboard to the backside of the mat. Glue the strips along the far edges of the mat, making sure that they aren't visible from the front of the artwork. Strips that are at least 1 inch narrower than the mat border won't show.

You can achieve even more depth by elevating both the artwork and the mats. The result is referred to as an elevated float. Attach the artwork to foamboard with V hinges that wrap around the top of the foamboard. Next, place cross supports on the hinge on the backside of the foamboard. When you initially attach the artwork to the foamboard, use an extra-long vertical strip of hinge material. Cross it at least two times on the backside of the foamboard to give the join additional support. Then glue the foamboard to the colored mat.

To create a float, cut the decorative mat windows to expose a bit of the background color field.

Here, the float has elevated mats for an added degree of depth.

If the artwork is large, it might drift off the elevating foamboard at the bottom edge. To eliminate this possibility, use an inverted V hinge to hold this edge against the foamboard.

Now that you've raised the art above the mats using V hinges, you may be wondering how to prevent the glass from touching the artwork. In order for the mats to support the glass, you must elevate them above the level of the artwork. Use double or triple thicknesses of foamboard scrap around the perimeter of the mats. Be sure to make the strips 1 inch narrower than the decorative top mat so the strips remain hidden.

To determine the correct placement of the elevated art piece, centering it on the colored field is essential. To help you find that location, take some measurements to calculate the width of the background color around the elevated image. Cut strips of scrap matting to that desired width, and then lay them out in an L shape. Then once you apply adhesive to the back of the foamboard, you can use this angle and placement to position the elevated artwork.

To make the depth produced via foamboard-core elevation more visible, pencils were inserted into the space between the mats.

A ¹/₄-inch thickness of foamboard was attached to the perimeter of both mats. This provides good support when the framing process begins.

Here, altered V hinges attach the art piece to the elevated foamboard. The hinge was pulled over the top of the foamboard support. Next, the tape was crossed on the backside to anchor the hinge into place.

ARCHIVAL MOUNTING

The artwork was hinged onto foamboard. Then the foamboard was then glued to the background color.

Here, the elevated art and mats provide additional depth. Artwork courtesy of Gretchen Curnes.

S HINGES

These hinges, which framers use less frequently than either T or V hinges, are designed to hold large, heavy pieces of art. S hinges closely resemble V hinges but differ in one important way. Unlike the top of the V hinge, which is folded back and anchored to render it invisible, the top of the S hinge is pushed through a slit in the backing material and then taped on the reverse side. S hinges are unusually strong because a long piece of hinge material supports the weight of the artwork. So the vertical pull is on this long hinge and the cross pieces used to hold the hinge in place on the rear side of the mat.

The materials you need to create S hinges include a ruler, a pencil, a knife to cut slits in the mat, acid-free adhesive, a brush, and rice paper torn to size.

NONARCHIVAL MOUNTING

Up to this point, all mounting methods have been archival quality. A few mounting methods, while not archival, are acid-free. These methods also limit the contact of adhesives and artworks.

WET MOUNTING

Years ago, wet mounting was the professionals' choice because it was the only method available. As a result, most mounted artworks were physically attached to a mounting material. This made it impossible to remove the piece of art without severely damaging it. Furthermore, the discoloring material the artwork was attached to, such as wood, caused additional irreparable damage. Today, such drawbacks can be overcome, but wet mounting isn't a popular mounting method.

With wet mounting, a mounting adhesive covers the back of the entire piece of art. Water-activated adhesives made from animal and vegetable sources were utilized long ago. Animal glues came from milk, blood, hide, and other tissues. Vegetable-based adhesives most often came from vegetable starches. Because of their success rates in terms of both application and reversal, vegetable adhesives were used regularly. Although new techniques have replaced the practice of overall mounting with such adhesives, starches are still used for hinging and infrequently for wet mounting.

You can make vegetable paste from a number of vegetable sources; however, rice and wheat starches are readily available, easy to work with, and most often used in conservation hinging. The primary problem with vegetable starches is keeping them fresh. Using a fungicide to retard spoilage can damage paper artwork. And while refrigeration prevents spoilage, it causes the starch and water to separate. Luckily, a wheat starch that has been prepared, redried, and packaged is available. All you have to do is rehydrate the starch with cold water.

Today, substitutes for rice and wheat starches include a variety of acid-free liquid adhesives that you can dispense and use without any preparation. These adhesives require new water-based materials that clean up easily. But beware: these adhesives aren't reversible.

If you want overall attachment, you can use a printmakers' brayer to roll a smooth coating of rice-starch adhesive over the entire backside of a piece of art. Don't let excess starch weep beneath the front of the artwork. Carefully lift the piece, and place it onto a suitable mounting material. After you allow the art to dry under even weight for 24 hours, you can proceed with the framing process.

Lineco liquid acid-free adhesive is used to prepare a print for mounting.

You can use rice starch, a natural material, to affix artwork to backing.

TAPE HINGES

The use of acid-free tape hinges, truly a fast-track discipline, represents another realm of mounting. These tapes consist of specially manufactured products that contain no damaging ingredients in their adhesives and are based on either lightweight linen or white paper. With only one exception, gummed linen tape, acid-free tapes are composed of materials that you can sometimes gently peel off the artwork. The best results occur when you slowly pull the tapes away from the artwork. Nevertheless, they always present the risk of damage to the artwork. Proceed with caution. (To reverse gummed linen tape, dampen it with water.)

Hinges can be made of less-expensive, acid-free paper tapes, as well as linen tapes. You apply them the same way you do rice-paper hinges: two pieces per hinge, and at least two hinges per artwork. Of course, you don't need any additional adhesive to attach them since the tapes are adhesive-backed. Because acid-free tape hinges don't require any drying time, they make artwork attachment go faster. Simply cut the tape, press, and continue the framing process. With these hinges you use less tape than you do when working with other paper hinges.

You can cut acid-free tape in strips to tape in artwork behind mats. Acid-free tape is also ideal for attaching photographs behind mats. The somewhat slick finish of the picture grabs on tight to the tape and holds well. Don't get carried away, though, and tape all around the image being matted. Paper needs to breathe, expanding and contracting with moisture changes. If taped all around, the paper will begin to puff and won't lie flat. Acid-free tape displays its weakest point when attaching soft, porous surfaces. To start with, the tape has a fairly low tack level. Dry, soft surfaces test its grip and holding power. And because excessive moisture can cause tapes to release, you should avoid using them on artwork that will hang in the kitchen or bathroom.

The real challenge of acid-free tape hinges is their removal, not their attachment. Most peel off the artwork without leaving any residue or causing damage when you exercise care. However, when exposed to extreme heat, and with time, they bond very tightly. So when you try to remove them, tearing and/or peeling of the art paper can occur. Use caution.

The first piece of a tape T hinge is in position.

The adhesive side of this V hinge is ready to be turned over onto a mounting surface.

DRY-TRANSFER ADHESIVES

These unique adhesive products, which are ideally suited for home framing, come in several forms. Each of these adhesives come in handy with posters, cards, collage compositions, photograph albums (no slipping), and almost any other paper item. Photographs hold tightly to the bonding agents in these adhesives.

But you must remember that while these dry-transfer adhesives have great holding power, they aren't archival-quality mounting materials. So for limited-edition artwork, you should consider one of the archival methods described earlier. Some dry-transfer adhesives, however, are acid-free and don't contain any chemicals that might discolor or damage artworks. You can find two types in most art-supply stores and craft centers: micro-thin adhesive film and adhesive droplets. These products have dramatically decreased the need for dangerous spray or messy liquid adhesives in the studio and the framing room.

Because dry-transfer adhesives are so convenient, you might want to try them. If you decide to buy dry-transfer adhesives, avoid storing these materials in areas of high humidity or high heat. A cool, dry storage area is recommended.

Despite the acid-free nature of some dry-transfer adhesives, you should remember that these products do attach the art to backing material. And whenever a piece of art is altered in any way, its economic value is greatly diminished. So mounting, for example, a limited-edition print or an original artwork with any type of adhesive that bonds the art to a surface isn't advisable.

MICRO-THIN ADHESIVE FILM

This ultra-thin film is coated on each side with adhesive and sandwiched between two sheets of release paper. Begin by peeling away either side of the release paper to expose the mounting material. When you've exposed an adequate amount of the film, carefully set the art on the film. Some repositioning is possible at this point of the mounting process. When you're pleased with the position of the art, simply close the top silicone-permeated sheet and press gently.

With the exception of photographs, you should burnish the art to the adhesive sheet with a flat, plastic burnishing tool. Like a kitchen spatula, the burnishing tool smooths the adhesive against the piece of art, releasing it from the second sheet of protective covering. Photographs have fragile surfaces, so you should use only your fingertips to burnish them, whichever type of adhesive you select. The edge of any burnishing tool could leave a crease or dent in the surface of the photograph.

Next, open the cover, trim away the excess mounting film, and peel off the back sheet of silicone paper. Although this is a bit inconvenient, you can save the film scraps and use them whenever their size is adequate. There is no opportunity for overlap with this material because the double thicknesses will show through some art pieces.

Place the art on the mounting choice. Once again, some repositioning is possible at this stage. When the art is correctly positioned, cover it with one of the original top silicone sheets. Then smooth it a final time with the flat burnishing tool. The artwork is now permanently mounted, exactly where you want it to be.

Double-sided film is packaged with silicone paper covers, which are used in the application process.

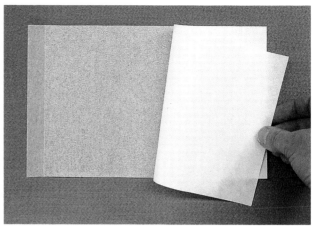

Dry-sheet adhesive has tiny adhesive droplets that are burnished onto the backside of the piece of art being mounted.

Here, a photograph is positioned on adhesive film. Photographs are especially well suited to this form of mounting.

Burnishing is recommended for all artworks except photographs. Their surface is fragile and may be damaged during the process.

Open the top silicone paper, and trim the mounting film to the edge of the art piece.

After you remove the second sheet of silicone from the backside of the art, place it on the mounting surface. Then lay a scrap of silicone paper over the top, and burnish a second time.

NONARCHIVAL MOUNTING

ADHESIVE DROPLETS

Another type of acid-free adhesive substance is dispensed in a fine mist of tiny, dry-glue droplets over the surface of a release paper. These droplets are then covered with a protective sheet. You apply these droplets in much the same way that you apply the double-faced film. Lift the top protective sheet and position the art right-side up on the droplet side of the sheet. Next, carefully clean any stray droplets off the protective covering sheet with a cotton ball or a paper towel. Lay the covering sheet over the art positioned on the droplet sheet. With either a printmakers' brayer, a scrap of mat board, or your fingertips, burnish the piece of art against the droplet side. A printmaker's brayer is a hard-rubber roller with a handle and looks like a tiny paint roller. This burnishing technique transfers the droplets to the backside of the art object.

Next, lift the covering sheet off the face of the artwork, and carefully peel the art item off the droplet sheet. The droplets have spread into a smooth, even coat of adhesive and have been transferred to the backside of the artwork. Now place the art on the mounting material of your choice, cover it with a protective sheet of silicone paper or the clean top sheet that came with the droplet page, and burnish it for a proper bond.

This droplet-type, dry-transfer adhesive sheet has one unique property. You can utilize every square inch of the material. As long as the adhesive droplets are covered and remain clean and uncontaminated, you can overlap, piece, and juggle them in order to use every speck. You won't have any waste.

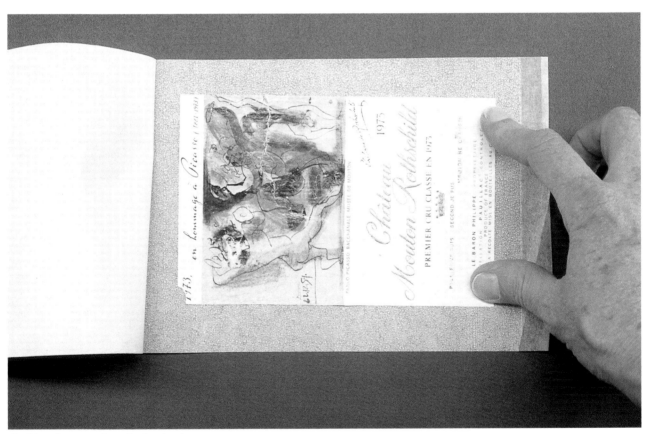

Position the artwork on the droplet sheet.

Burnish the backside of the adhesive sheet to the back of the artwork.

Peel the artwork off the adhesive sheet. The adhesive is then transferred to the back of the art.

Position the artwork on a background surface, cover it with a scrap of silicone paper, and burnish for permanence.

MATERIALS WITH LIMITATIONS

When finances are low, time is short, or caution isn't being exercised, artists and home decorators are tempted to use the first material they can locate that will work for the mounting job at hand. Since mounting art isn't a visible part of the framing process, it is one area in which many people use products that cause trouble. Such problems may not occur quickly, but at some time in the future, improper mounting methods will become a challenge to correct. You should be familiar with a few of the common pitfalls associated with using materials not designed for a specific application.

TAPES

Many different kinds of tapes are available on the market, and most of them do a great job of meeting the manufacturers' claims. You can buy: tapes for packaging and for attaching paper to paper; reinforced tapes for extra strength and heavy-duty uses; removable, repositionable tapes for use on paper; duct tape, which can bond almost anything to anything; masking tape, which you can use hundreds of ways; electrical tape, for wiring; and regular office tape, like cellophane tape. All of these tapes are indispensable, but not one is intended for use in quality art framing.

These tapes aren't suitable for framing for various reasons. First, they're designed only for temporary use. Granted, this "temporary" usage may last a rather long time, but almost all eventually dry out and give way. Second, they contain high amounts of destructive materials that at best cause severe staining and sticky residue. You can use these tapes when putting protective coverings on framed pieces of art, packaging framed items, and sealing cartons. But none of these tapes is manufactured or recommended for use when tape will come in direct contact with artwork.

One reason why you should avoid them is the fugitive qualities of their glues. Over time, the adhesives dry out, begin to turn to powder, and lose any holding power they had originally. Two negative outcomes result. First, the piece of art will slip out of place when the grip of the adhesive lets go. This looks bad. Second, the artwork might fall to the bottom of the frame, and its edges might be damaged.

More damaging than the slipping is the staining residue that the dried tape leaves behind. And in the process of changing from its original white or cream color to golden brown, the dried adhesive discolors the paper artwork as well.

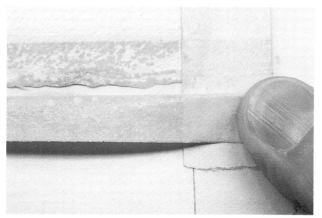

Here, the alarming effects of a tape used to attach an original watercolor are visible. The adhesive has turned golden brown, and the tape is brittle.

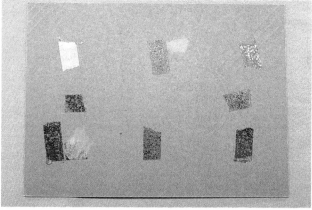

The backside of this artwork has heavy, sticky deposits from tape used to hold an acetate cover in place.

The only way to solve this problem is to have a conservator eliminate this stain. This procedure is quite costly. But staining is the lesser of your problems if, in addition, the tape has started to attack the art. Certain tapes can actually begin to destroy the paper itself. In fact, tape and nonarchival glues can literally dissolve the paper fibers, resulting in perforations.

At best, even for short-term holding, the tapes leave a sticky residue when you remove them. This residue is difficult to eliminate without the use of a strong solvent. Keep in mind, though, that you have no guarantee that the solvent itself won't result in damage equal to or more devastating than that the tape residue causes.

You can easily and automatically avoid all of these situations by simply choosing a quality tape designed for contact with any paper artwork. If you use a special, yet affordable, framing tape that is acid-free, you'll never have to be concerned with such problems again. These tapes are designated as safe, with a neutral pH, and are actually recommended for attaching any artwork when this particular type of adhesive is needed.

Several companies make these special tapes, which are available at art-supply stores, through catalog art-supply facilities and occasionally at discount arts-and-crafts-supply stores. The price of the tapes is low when you consider that the purchase of any one of them eliminates worry. Two types of tape are specifically manufactured for the framing industry. One is a special double-sided sticky tape and one is a frame-sealing tape.

DOUBLE-SIDED TAPE

This kind of tape consists of a thin strip of adhesive attached to a strip of silicone paper for easy application. You can use double-sided tape for various tasks, but it isn't recommended for attaching artwork to mats or backing. To use double-sided tape, simply apply it sticky side down, and then pull away the silicone paper strip. You can purchase an applicator gun that dispenses the sticky strip and collects the protective paper. This one-step, fast-action tool is a big help for framers, regardless of their level of involvement. A tape gun is great for applying tape to join mats, prepare the frame for a dust cover, stack foamboard elevations, create glass-elevation strips, attach foamboard for increased support, and join any paper to any other paper.

Be aware that double-sided tape isn't an archival, acid-free material; it contains contaminants. Never use it where it might come in contact with artwork. You can, however, use it hundreds of ways. The applicator gun costs around $60. The special silicone-paper-backed tape for the tape gun usually costs less than $5 per roll.

Double-sided tape is dispensed on silicone paper strips. It is ideal for joining paper to paper or mat to mat.

A tape gun is designed to dispense the tape and to take up the waste strip on an inside spool. Both working with the gun and changing the tape are easy to manage.

MATERIALS WITH LIMITATIONS

FRAME-SEALING TAPE

This tape was designed especially for sealing a work of art in a frame. After you fit the artwork into the frame, you apply sealing tape around the edges of the art. This seal will be important if artworks are to be displayed in high-humidity areas. This tape offers more protection from moisture infiltration. Although using this tape isn't necessary for every framing project, you should utilize it when the situation calls for it. Seal the art with the tape right after you affix the art in the frame via nails or points (see page 121). Once you've completed this step, protect the piece with a dust cover.

You can use sealing tape on metal molding, too. Simply position the tape around the back hardware channel. Make sure that the tape comes in contact with both the frame and the backing material.

Frame-sealing tape is the only acid-free tape made specifically for framing. Backed with a peel-off paper, the tape is self-adhering.

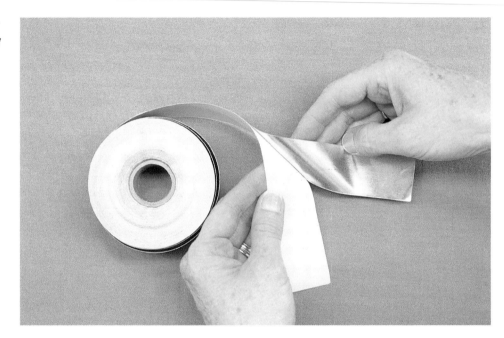

Sealing tape serves as a moisture barrier on the inside of wooden frames by covering the seam around the artwork. You place it over the points or brads that hold the artwork in position.

SPRAY MOUNTING

An effective way to mount inexpensive posters or other large, paper art pieces is with a spray adhesive. Many brands are designed to hold any paper item in place for an indefinite period of time. Spray adhesives are particularly helpful in creating fabric-covered mats. First, spray the adhesive on the mat's surface, and then apply the fabric to this sticky side of the mat. This method works on all but the thinnest fabrics. Match the product's holding power to the job you're asking the adhesive to do.

Spray mounting has less of a tendency to release its hold than other forms of mounting. This is because you coat the entire backside of the artwork with the spray adhesive before mounting. This type of adhesive application makes the gripping power quite strong.

Proper application of spray adhesive is essential to achieve a flat, evenly mounted paper artwork. The simple spray pattern of slightly overlapping passes from side to side and then from top to bottom gives an even mist of adhesive. No buildup or puddling occurs along the edges when you begin and end your spraying pattern off the surface of the print.

After spraying, lift the artwork by its outer edges. Turn it over, and roll the sticky side down against an oversized mounting board. Carefully smooth out any bubbles with a side-to-side motion of your hands.

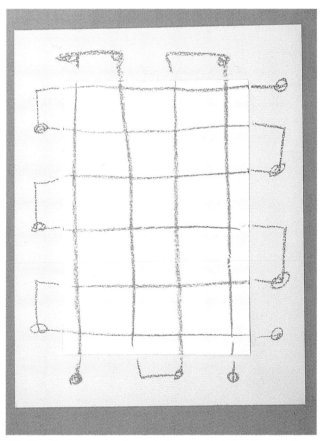

The blue lines represent the vertical passes. A light mist in each direction ensures even distribution without edge buildup.

After spraying an artwork, lift the piece by the edges, turn it over, and roll it onto the mounting surface.

Next, cover the front of the art with clean craft paper or some other protective material. Place a large, smooth surface over the stack; a scrap of Plexiglas or laminate is ideal. It is always advisable to allow the spray-mounted artwork to dry under a weight, such as books, bricks, or bags filled with beans or stones, for 24 hours.

A few parts of the spray-mounting procedure can be tricky. Suppose, for example, that when you spray the backside of a print, you accidentally allow a buildup of adhesive at the edge. Then when you place the piece under a weight, the excess oozes out from the edge and gets on the front of the artwork. To eliminate this sticky spot, you can use Adhesive Release (see Resources on page 142). This product, which resembles a dry-cleaning fluid, removes glue residue while making only a minimal change in the print's surface. Gently apply Adhesive Release with a cotton swab. It dries almost instantly, so no removal is necessary. After the weighted drying time, trim the excess foamboard to size. Proceed with the framing plan of your choice.

You might encounter another common problem. If after mounting a print with spray adhesive, you notice a pocket of air trapped under the art, you have to remove it. This problem sometimes happens when you work with large pieces of art. The easiest way to remove the air pocket is to pierce a hole in the mounting board behind the bubble. Then put a weight on the spot, and let it remain in place for another 24 hours. This should eliminate all traces of the bubble.

You should always practice caution when using spray adhesives. They can be harmful to your health. In addition, they broadcast a mist of sticky residue that extends many feet around the sprayed item. In fact, only about 60 percent of what you spray actually attaches itself to the art. The remainder is in the air you're breathing, floating around you. So cover all adjacent areas to prevent excess spray from accumulating on them. The best place to use spray adhesives is outside. Spread out newspaper or craft paper on your terrace or driveway or in your backyard, for example, and protect your furnishings.

Put a protective covering over the spray-coated art, and then let the item dry under a clean weight for 24 hours.

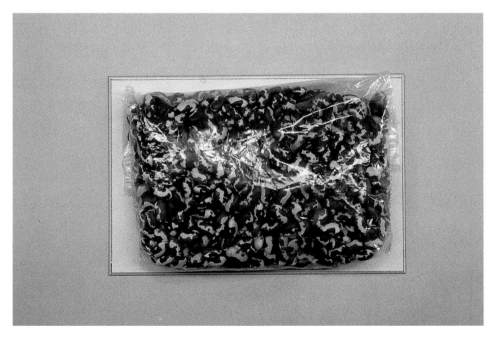

MOUNTING SPECIALTY ITEMS

Some of the most creative and fun projects involve mounting and framing what I call "challenge" works. These projects include heirloom fabric pieces, photographs, three-dimensional objects, pastels, and special displays for watercolors. Each piece of art presents an interesting design and requires specific application strategies. You can use the examples discussed here as a jumping-off place, customizing many of the ideas as you gain experience. Let your creativity run wild as you contemplate the unusual items you want to display.

FABRIC ARTWORKS

Home framers are becoming increasingly interested in artwork done on woven fabric. This piece of fabric art can be anything from an antique sampler or tapestry to a contemporary cross stitch or batik. Each fabric poses a specific challenge. Some stitchery fabrics, such as linen, are tightly woven, while others, like loosely woven cottons and blends used in embroidery work, are soft and stretchy. Many others have an irregular thread so that the weave has texture, while others are smooth and tightly woven with precise linear patterns.

You can present fabric artworks in a number of ways. Two of the most common methods offer the fabric piece support and protection from rapid deterioration. Each technique requires simple materials that are readily available. Foam-covered mounting boards are no longer recommended because over time the foam breaks down and turns to powder. Sticky boards contain discoloring and damaging materials and can cause irreparable harm to treasured stitchery works in a brief amount of time.

"How Many Fish Do You See?" Velvet McFeeters. Mixed aqua media. Because this artwork was mounted via the float technique, the deckled edges of the paper become part of the finished look.

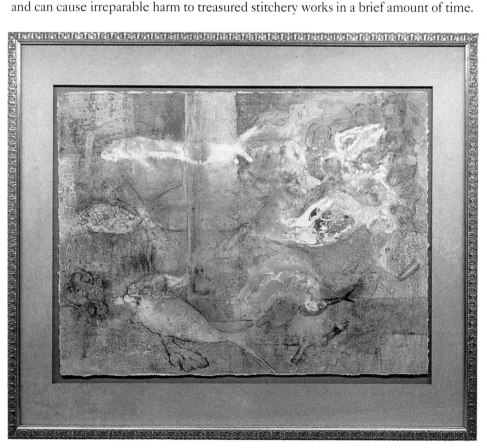

MOUNTING SPECIALTY ITEMS

The proper presentation of fabric artworks is important for two aesthetic reasons. First, if you have an heirloom sampler, for example, you'll want to mount it so that the entire image is clearly visible. Second, you'll want the borders to be straight and the weave to be even when the sampler is viewed hanging on the wall.

One mounting method takes these elements into consideration and provides the best chance of a straight, even mounting, as well as good life expectancy. Everyday dressmakers' straight pins are the magic ingredient in a successful stretching and mounting of a fabric artwork. Inexpensive and easy to find, they hold well for a long time. In fact, they function as well as any professional stretching pins used in the custom-framing industry.

Before you begin mounting a fabric artwork, you should decide whether it needs to be cleaned. Keep in mind, though, that washing it can cause some threads to release their colors and ruin the stitchery. If you think that washing is necessary before stretching because of hoop marks or soil, use an organic liquid soap. This product is available at health-food stores. Use cool water, and avoid wringing out the art piece. Dry it flat on a towel, and press it from the backside when it is almost dry.

Before you actually start working with any fabric artwork, be sure to wash your hands. Carefully measure the fabric piece. Allow for the slight give in most fabrics and any tightly stitched spots that might resist stretching. Take your time with this step. If the fabric is loosely woven, measure while slightly pulling it.

The single, most important element of the stretching and mounting of fabric works is the squareness of the mounting foamboard. If the foamboard is cut "off square," the fabric piece will never appear straight along the edges. With a T square or a carpenter's corner square, cut the mounting material carefully. Doing your best to cut the foamboard on square will make the project much easier to complete.

Cover the surface of the foamboard with a single thickness of rag mat board or all-rag barrier paper. This prevents the fabric from coming in contact with even the low contaminants in the foamboard. Locate the center, top to bottom, of the art piece. Place a pin at that point on the top and bottom of the piece. Follow the grain of the fabric to find the exact corners, and pin them. Fill in along the edges, easing and stretching when necessary. Space the pins evenly, about every 1/4 inch. Pull all excess fabric to the back, and sew with a criss-cross thread pattern to hold the extra material in place. This is called couching.

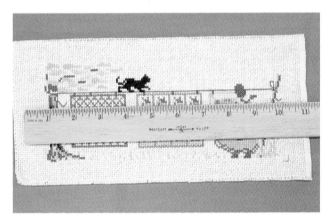

Measure the size you want the fabric piece to be when the stretching is complete.

To provide extra protection, cover the foamboard with all-rag artists' paper. You may opt to use acid-free foamboard.

Begin the stretch by locating the fabric's center, top, and bottom.

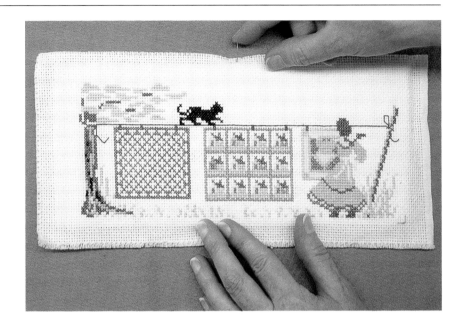

Locate and pin all four corners.

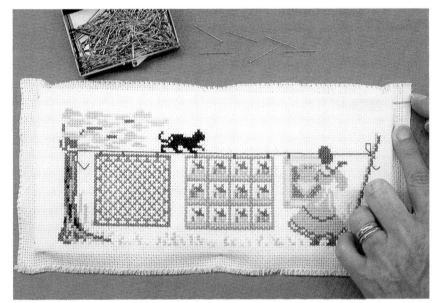

Place the pins every ¹/₄ inch to ensure a tight hold.

At this point, you can either frame the work or mat it with an all-rag mat. The mat will cover a bit of the edge of the stitchery. When you cut and place the mat on the mounted fabric artwork, you might need to adjust the pull in an area along any of the sides of the mat window. To do this, simply release the pins in the area, and then stretch the fabric again. This slight adjustment is sometimes necessary because the mounting board might be slightly off square, or because the mat window has a tiny discrepancy.

Next, position the mat over the fabric piece. Carefully turn the entire package over. Then fill in around the stretched fabric work, using scraps of foamboard, from the edge of the stretched work to the edge of the mat. Use double-sided sticky tape to hold the foamboard scraps in place. When you complete this step, you can continue the project with a glass and frame.

Although purists don't put stitchery works under glass, professional framers recommend doing so. Glass protects the artwork from the dust in homes and the pollutants in the atmosphere. It also extends the life of the stitchery. Glass shouldn't have direct contact with the fabric. It can trap moisture (see page 55 for more information on elevating glass).

On the backside of the needlework, couch the excess fabric. Begin with a top-to-bottom crisscross pattern.

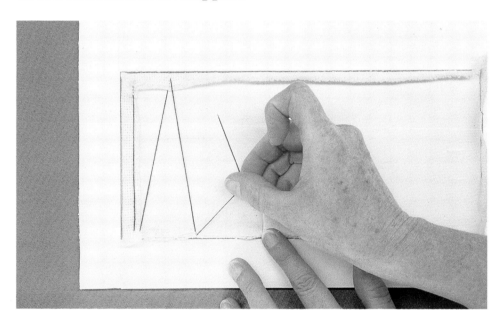

Complete with an end-to-end crisscross pattern. Although maintaining even edges is difficult, you can use couching to stretch an artwork onto a mounting board.

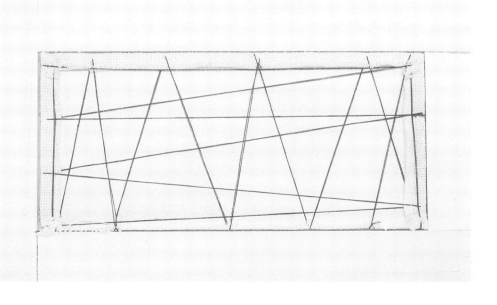

With the mat in place, check for a straight weave along its edges. Adjust wherever necessary.

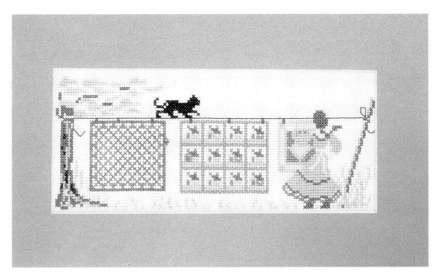

Use double-sided tape to hold foamboard strips around the stretched needlework. This not only fills in around the piece, but also supports the mat.

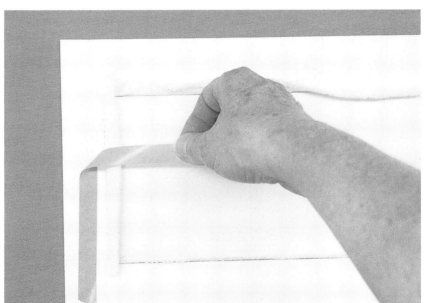

Place scrap strips around the needlework to fill all the space between its edge and the outside edge of the mat.

PHOTOGRAPHS

Pictures are one of the most popular items to mat and frame. When you decide to frame photographs, you need to consider a few facts about them. Before you start any actual mounting, determine exactly where you want to place your photograph on the mounting board. After you make this decision, carefully trace light registration marks around all four corners with a pencil to help you properly place the photograph. This guarantees the exact position for slight edge overlap by the mats.

You can mount photographs, the first step in their presentation, in a number of ways. One method that has been used for years is spray mounting with special aerosol spray adhesives designed for photographs. Once again, you should exercise caution with these sprays. Other products that mount photographs perfectly are the adhesive films and dry-transfer adhesive sheets described earlier. Each does a great job and is both easy and safe to use.

You can purchase special photographic mounting corners, an updated version of the old, photo-album corners, at art-supply stores; you can also order these products from art-supply catalogs. The new corners are pressure-sensitive, transparent, and ready to use. They employ an acid-free adhesive and won't damage photographs.

Be aware that a photograph should never actually touch the glass in a frame. The reason for avoiding such direct contact is easy to understand. Any rapid temperature change in the glass's surface causes it to "perspire." This problem occurs most frequently in the bathroom, the kitchen, and unusual wall locations.

Before mounting a photograph onto the desired material, decide where you want to position it.

Once the adhesive is on the picture, all you have left to do is to set the photograph within the corner marks.

For example, if you hang a framed photograph on the wall in a hallway near a window where light crosses over it, the fast, repetitive warming and cooling will produce condensation. The moisture is trapped in the frame, with nowhere to go but onto the surface of the picture.

The quickest and easiest way to raise the glass off the surface of the image is to use a mat. This slight elevation eliminates any possibility of an adhesion problem. Even in the extreme case of a rapid warming and cooling of the photograph, the moisture has a chance to dissipate before causing severe damage.

If you choose to frame an image without a mat, you can still elevate the glass off the picture's surface. To accomplish this, attach thin strips of black-core mat board to the glass around its perimeter. These strips, which elevate the glass equivalent to a mat border, enable the picture to be displayed with glazing protection, but without a full mat to hold the glass away from the surface.

Attaching the strips may sound difficult, but a professional trick simplifies the process. Cut the strips from a scrap of black-core mat that is longer than the longest side of the frame. Place several passes of double-faced tape directly adjacent to one another down the length of the black-core base. Don't remove the protective paper covering. When you need elevating strips, just measure and cut ⅛-inch strips from the tape-covered area of the black-core mat. Peel the protective covering off the thin strips, and position the sticky strips at the outside edges of the glass. This is the easiest way to cut elevation strips and glue them into place. After you cut, peel, and place the strips, flip the glass and set it over the photograph.

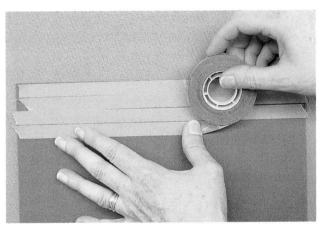

When using glass-elevation strips, begin by putting numerous passes of double-sided tape in place.

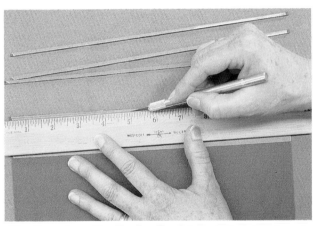

Measure and cut strips that are approximately ⅛ inch wide and the full length of the glass you're elevating.

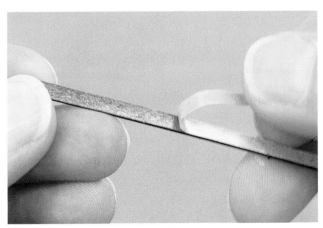

Peel off the protective paper, and align the strip with the edge of the glass.

Press the strip on the inside of the glass right at the outer edges. Strips need to be positioned all around the glass.

THREE-DIMENSIONAL ARTWORK

You can mount, frame, and display virtually any piece of artwork. Framing collectibles often enables you to enjoy them everyday, rather than store them. People often consider common possessions that once belonged to family members a generation ago to be decorative. Such three-dimensional items as coins, eyeglasses, baby clothes, football jerseys, security blankets, bouquets, toys, political memorabilia, and guns are treasured and framed. A few professional tips will help give you perfect results.

Suppose that you want to display a handmade tile. For this simple three-dimensional artwork, you'll mount it on a colored field. One of the easiest ways to frame any three-dimensional piece of art, it is also one of the most delightful.

When you measure the tile, calculate the border widths and the amount of mounting-board color you want to show. For a typical tile or any similar-sized piece of art, 1 inch is probably the maximum amount of base color you would show. Here, you'll use a $1/2$-inch mat around the tile. Cut the decorative top mat to size. Mark the window, and recheck the dimensions by setting the tile on the area that will be cut away. If it is centered, cut the opening. If it isn't centered, check your calculations, remark, and cut the opening.

Next, attach the solid-colored background mat to a foamboard backing using any strong glue. This supports the mat and makes the finished piece stable. Place strips of mat board around the tile to indicate its position. Use silicone adhesive to hold the tile in place. Silicone adhesive is great for bonding nonporous materials to any mounting surface. Use an adequate amount of silicone, being careful not to place the flow too close to the edges of the tile. Otherwise, when you press the tile into position, the silicone might ooze around the edge of the tile and show. Remove the positioning strips, press the tile into place, and allow the assembly to dry for 24 hours.

When it is time to continue, complete the top decorative mat that will appear around the tile. Glue strips of foamboard scrap to the backside of the mat to elevate it above the face of the tile. This particular handmade tile requires a double thickness of foamboard for proper elevation. Glue the elevated mat to the background mat for stability. All you have left to do is to install a glazing choice and put the package into a frame.

The three-dimensional objects that you can successfully mount this way include plates, guns, knives, political badges, coins, plaques, leaves—virtually any other solid, opaque item. If the item that you want to mount isn't perfectly straight along the edges, measure the widest part of it. Then adjust its position until you center it on the background. If you're mounting an irregularly shaped item, a small piece of siliconed foamboard under it might help to even out its frontal appearance. Use silicone to attach both the foamboard to the background mat and the object to the foamboard. Hidden support and attachment are the marks of a professional presentation.

Whatever piece of art you're working with, the first step in framing is to measure. Here, after you measure the tile, you have to calculate the borders you want to use around this three-dimensional object.

After cutting the mat and backing but before attaching the tile, set the tile in the marking for the mat window. This is a fast way to check your calculations.

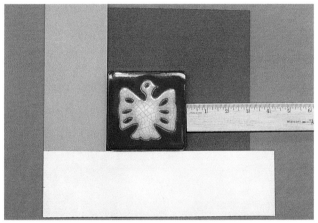

Cut strips of scrap mat board to help position the tile in the center of the background color.

Apply silicone along the edges of the tile and a bit extra at each corner.

Once the tile has dried completely in 24 hours, remove the indicator strips.

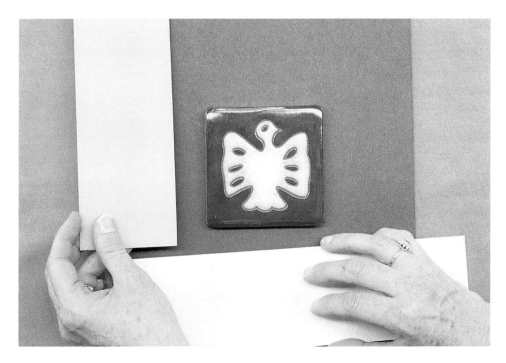

Attach double foamboard strips to the back of the mat in order to elevate it above the tile.

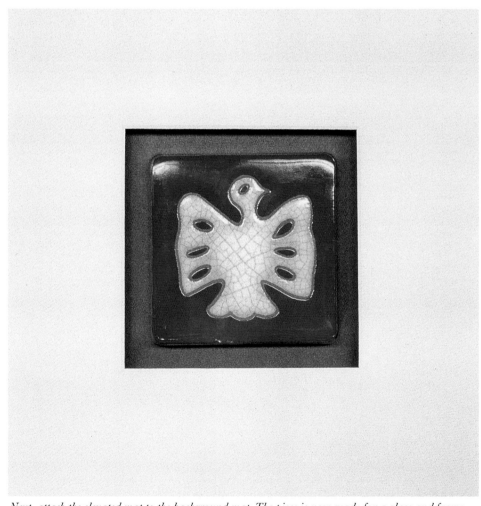

Next, attach the elevated mat to the background mat. The piece is now ready for a glass and frame.

Collections of insects pose an especially interesting display challenge. As a child, you might have collected insects for a school project. Chances are that you pinned these insects onto a board and turned them in for a science project. This method is still a viable way to display insects. Use dressmakers' straightpins to secure the insect. You might need several pins to hold the specimen in place.

You can mount fragile items, such as feathers and pressed flowers and leaves, with tiny deposits of silicone. This adhesive not only holds the object exactly where you want it, but also lifts it off the background. The silicone doesn't cause deterioration or discoloration. Be careful when you apply silicone because any smears will appear to be oily spots, thereby ruining the look of the finished mounting. Also, silicone adhesive slowly turns from clear to golden brown when exposed to ultraviolet (UV) light over the course of several months. This is another reason why your application must be precise. If silicone shows slightly, let the area dry completely. Then use an X-Acto knife to cut away the excess.

You can use silicone adhesive to mount thin, fragile natural items. It not only attaches them to the background material, but also gives them some lift.

This collection of maple leaves has been under glass for more than eight years. The silicone used to hold the leaves in place hasn't changed their appearance.

MOUNTING SPECIALTY ITEMS

Mounting with silicone isn't right for all projects. This is particularly true when the three-dimensional object is made out of fabric or some other soft material. These items include a wedding veil, a christening dress, a doily, a collectors' sports jersey, a collection of antique handkerchiefs, a hat, and a pair of booties—any one of thousands of items. You'll need to consider another mounting method for these projects. Sewing might be your best choice. Sewing can be reversed in the future if color changes are required and doesn't damage the material. This is the best way to exhibit the items in this unique "posture."

Before you start the actual mounting procedure, you should wash any white cloth items you plan to frame with an organic cleaner. Then set them out in bright sunlight to "bleach" them in order to achieve a clear, clean, vibrant white. If you'll be working with fabric artwork, press the pieces before you sew them into place. Wrinkles appear even more pronounced in a frame.

Suppose you want to mount a doily on a colored surface. Begin by measuring the item. You might need to stretch the doily a bit to eliminate any puckers or misshapen designs. As you do your calculations, add the amount of surround color desired and then add the border widths. Once you finish these size calculations, cut the solid sheet of mat color, the foamboard backing, and the mat from which you'll cut a window.

To sew the doily down, make pilot holes in the mat with a push pin. Sew through the holes, entering and exiting through the same hole. The amount of sewing required to hold the doily in the correct shape is hard to estimate. Remember that the doily position is vertical when displayed, and any loose area of the doily will sag. In this case, too much is better than too little sewing. When you've sewn the doily in place, cut the window in the top decorative mat. Circular-shaped items offer a great opportunity to use circular mat windows (see page 72).

Mounting some three-dimensional objects may initially seem difficult. For example, you want to mount a pistol, but its chamber is so thick that the gun barrel droops. To solve this problem, countersink the chamber into the surround mat and into the foam backing. This will help with the barrel droop. Another challenging project involves a pair of old eyeglasses that your great-grandfather wore. Your first thought might be to attach them with silicone. But this isn't a good idea. Because the glasses are so thin, the silicone is bound to show. Examine them carefully, looking for places where you can sew them to the backing. Use transparent nylon thread; it disappears into the seams, cracks, and hinges of items being mounted.

Still feeling nostalgic, you regard the flag that once flew over the family lake house as a treasure. You have it framed and hanging on display in the den. But the fringe around the top edge doesn't lay flat in the frame, and you want to fix it. Your only option is to sew down every piece of fringe along the top and sides. Although this project will be time-consuming, the effort it takes will pay off when you see how good the flag looks when you're done.

Perhaps one day you decide that your collection of old coins would be perfect for the game room in your house. You want to mount them so that they appear to be floating off the background. To achieve this effect, cut small pieces of foamboard, and use silicone to attach them to the coins. Next, attach the foamboard pieces to the background with silicone. For small coins, a tall dollop of silicone may be sufficient.

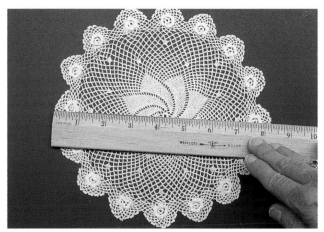

The first step is to measure the size of the doily.

Begin the sewing process by stretching the doily where necessary to achieve the desired shape.

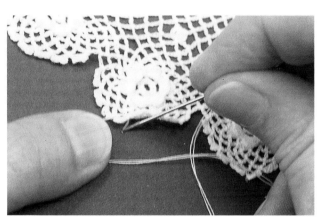

Use pushpins to hold the doily in position while you sew. Then sew through the holes that the pushpins made.

Enter and exit through the same hole.

Round shapes lend themselves perfectly to circular mat windows. Cut a top mat with the appropriate borders, and then elevate and attach it to the background mat.

PASTELS AND OTHER POWDERY ARTWORKS

Artworks made with pastels, charcoal, and chalk pose some of the most difficult mounting and handling challenges in framing. Pastel artists are quite selective, carefully choosing the colors that provide a soft, velvety look. They don't work the particles of powder into the surface. In addition, the pastels don't have many bonding properties.

Few pastel artists would consider spraying any type of fixative over their work because the character of the material might change. But since the surface is dry and only marginally attached to the ground material, it is subject to disturbance. If the surface is touched, bumped, tapped, or blown across, it lets go of many minute particles. The fragile balance of material compatibility and surface hold represents a framer's nightmare. Fixatives, however, prevent the powders from lifting off or smearing before the artwork is framed. And after the piece of art is under glass, fixatives continue to hold the particles in place. But any moist spray will cause some of the particles to disappear. This change is subtle, and given the fixatives' overall holding power and protective qualities, seems a small price to pay.

To protect powdery artworks, store them in a dust-free area, with a sheet of tissue paper sitting lightly over the image. When you start the project, frame the piece as quickly as possible—without, of course, sacrificing quality. Don't roll the drawing. If you do, the image will transfer to the backside of the work and smear, possibly destroying the piece. Also, don't blow on the artwork with any type of power blower in an effort to remove excess pastel or charcoal dust. Conservation mounting is recommended for powdery artwork because you can complete a conservation mounting without excessively handling the artwork.

Keep in mind the following valuable framing tips. First, you must always put powdery pieces of art under glass. Otherwise, the artwork's appearance will be adversely affected over time by being rubbed, bumped, and/or touched.

Plan to use at least one mat around the image. Then, by elevating the mat (or mats) with foamboard strips, you provide a channel for the dust particles to fall into. Also, never use Plexiglas or any other acrylic or plastic glazing material on powdery artworks. These glazing products are charged with static electricity and attract dust and debris, including powder from the artwork.

You might also be wondering if working with mixed media that includes pastel, charcoal, or chalk presents the same framing challenges. Any art piece that contains powdery markings is subject to smearing. So use care when framing such an artwork, whether it utilizes a single medium or mixed media.

Pastels are one of the most difficult items to frame. Their surfaces, which are a continual source of powder, smear easily.

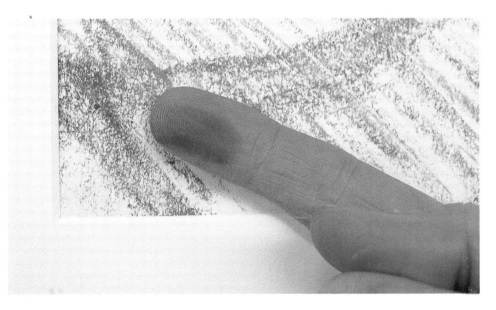

WATERCOLORS

High-quality watercolor papers are made by hand from a slurry, which is a thick bath of fibers contained in a large vat. As screens, or molds, are pulled through the slurry, they collect fibers. This slurry is actually the paper in a liquid state. Then when the water is squeezed out of the fibers, they join to form the sheet. From slurry to completed sheet, the paper has a kinship with water. In many watercolor techniques, the paper on which the painting is completed is resoaked in water for extended periods of time. This enables the paper to absorb moisture and to prepare for colors to be washed onto the surface. The soaking prevents hard edges and yields soft, mingled colors. This is why the paper must be dry before framing, and why you should display watercolor paintings away from excessive humidity. The paper's absorption quality can help you flatten a "puffy" watercolor painting.

Allow the finished watercolor to dry thoroughly. When the painting is ready, turn it face down on a dry, smooth, nonporous work surface. Next, lightly mist the backside of the work with clean, distilled water. Then turn the painting face up, and cover it with a smooth, flat surface, such as a sheet of Plexiglas, a piece of laminate, or clear glass. Apply weight, such as bricks or books—anything that will provide a uniform pressing. Leave the assembly in this position for at least 24 hours.

When the artwork is dry and flat, mount, mat, and frame it as soon as possible. Once you complete the framing, seal the backside of the frame with frame-sealing tape or artists' tape for extra protection against moisture absorption. Avoid hanging your treasured originals in humid areas, like bathrooms and kitchens. If, however, you feel compelled to hang the art in a wooden frame in such a space, try a professional framer's secret. Put a second dust cover on top of the first.

When you work with watercolors, remember that a float mount is often an ideal way to display these paintings. By attaching the image to a colored field via invisible hinges and letting the field become part of the overall design, you create an element of depth. For an even more striking look, keep in mind the elevated float mount.

When you have a watercolor on paper that has cut edges, you can achieve a dimensional look by slightly adapting a traditional mounting approach. For this method to be successful, you must be able to cover at least $1/2$ inch of the watercolor's image area on all four sides. The process begins with conservation-corner or hinge-type mounting. After you make mat choices, cut the windows precisely. But before the mats become a part of the presentation, elevate them above the image area with one thickness of foamboard. You can also add one thickness of foamboard between each of the mats. The resulting look has far greater depth and dimension than traditional matting and watercolor presentations.

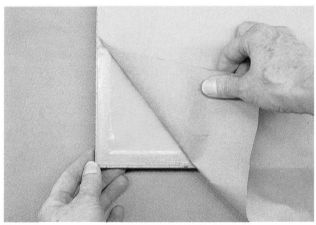

For extra protection against moisture, put a double dust cover over the powdery artwork.

When the edges of a watercolor aren't evenly deckled, you're limited to traditional mounting styles in which the mats are directly against the edges of the work.

CHAPTER 4

MATTING

Matting materials are available in dozens of colors, textures, and fabrics, including lace, suede, simulated leathers, and metallic finishes. This great variety makes coordinating the matting and the artwork easy. So if you are an artist, you can continue the creative process after you finish an artwork by making all of your own mounting, matting, and framing decisions. You can be in complete control of the final look of your work—in other words, the entire package. If you collect art and want to frame your collection, you can reveal your creativity by planning and executing mounting, matting, and framing with choices that are uniquely your own.

Because of the range of materials on the market, you can mat any artwork in hundreds of ways. When you do your own presentation and select the colors you want to emphasize, you control the outcome. In addition to the satisfaction that comes from seeing a project through from start to finish, you can also enjoy the economical aspect. It is far less expensive to do your own matting, whether you opt for simple, elegant matting or flashy designer combinations. You can devote as much time and energy into a project as you wish.

Simply by offsetting the mat windows in this double-matted photograph and including a few collected leaves, I was able to transform "St. Louis Maples" into a dynamic piece.

MATTING MATERIALS

Before you begin learning how to effectively mat your artwork, you should be familiar with the various types of matting. Mat boards come in three sizes. The highest number of surface and core colors and texture choices are available in 32×40-inch sheets. This is considered the regular, or standard, size mat board. Some surface and core colors and textures are available in sheets that measure 40×60 inches, and a very limited number of special museum mats are available in 48×96-inch sheets.

Not surprisingly, regular mat board is the most commonly used type, by both professional and amateur framers. This material is made of wood pulp, which ordinarily is an unstable, quick-to-yellow, and short-lived material that reacts quickly to the effects of UV light. Recently, though, the production of regular mat boards was changed to include a calcium buffering agent. This agent acts like an antacid, neutralizing the acidity of the mats and making them useful for almost any matting project. Even though regular mat boards aren't considered conservation quality, they change their look and chemical makeup slowly.

Regular mat boards are made up of three layers. The top colored layer is unbuffered. The inner core and the backing paper, however, are buffered and acid-free. This matting is easy to cut and is made without impurities, so the cut edges are always neat and uniform in coloration. The least expensive of all matting materials, regular mat boards are available at art-supply stores and discount art-material stores, as well as through mail-order catalogs.

As you make your selections, keep in mind that all-rag matting is different from regular matting in several ways. Because the core of all-rag matting is made up entirely of processed cotton fibers, it is pure and naturally acid-free. All-rag mats, like regular mats, are composed of three layers. But in all-rag mats, the colored surface is buffered, the white core is all-cotton and acid-free, and the bottom layer is all-rag and acid-free. (Black-core, all-rag matting is also available.) When you cut and expose a white, all-rag core mat, it will remain white for a long period of time. All this attention to archival quality makes all-rag mats the best choice for framing collectibles or heirlooms.

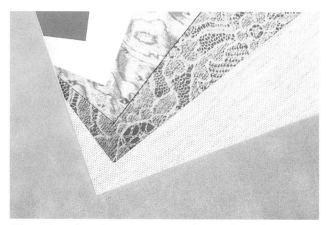

The variety of matting textures, core colors, surface colors, and specialty finishes available offer something to go with every artwork.

Over time, mat boards react to the UV illumination they're exposed to. Here, the effect of UV light on two old mats with a wood-pulp base is obvious when they're placed next to a new rag mat.

MATTING
MATERIALS

The price of all-rag matting is roughly double to triple that of regular matting. The additional expense is justified when you consider the degree of uncompromised quality they offer. But be aware that with all-rag matting, your color choices are limited to about ⅓ the number regular matting offers. Most art-supply stores and catalog-order centers offer all-rag mats.

Museum mat board is the purest, all-rag matting material available. It consists of four identical layers joined with a natural, organic adhesive. These layers are bonded under pressure to form a uniform sheet of material that appears to be a single, thick piece. So when you make beveled cuts in a museum rag board, all surfaces are the same color.

Color selection in museum boards is quite small. You can choose from several shades of white and cream, or a rich jet black. Theoretically, you can bond a colored, all-rag artists' paper to the surface of a museum mat. But the end result would be so similar to an all-rag mat that this isn't a viable alternative.

As you make matting choices, avoid the temptation to select colors that match the room the artwork will go in if those colors aren't present in the piece. The art will never look as good as it could. Ideally, the colors best suited to the image will also work well in the room. And keep in mind that the use of a single mat that has a specialty, colored core is like getting two mats for the price of one. This single-mat option is both economically astute and aesthetically appealing.

All-rag mats have pure white cores. Other types of mats have black cores, and a few even have pastel cores.

TABLE-TOP CUTTERS

If hand-cutting isn't your preference, you can try one of the various table-top cutters that greatly simplify mat cutting. Their range of features and sophistication is surprising. All of the table-top cutters on the market offer beveled cutting, easy-grip cutting heads, adjustable border widths, and simple blade replacement. Additionally, each device comes with thorough instructions and support material.

In the higher-cost range for amateur cutters, you can purchase a table-top cutter capable of cutting down full-sized sheets of mat board or backing material. Some of these cutters come with other great features as well. These include mat-cutting stops that preset mat measurements for speedy repetitions and the ability to accurately measure and cut down these materials.

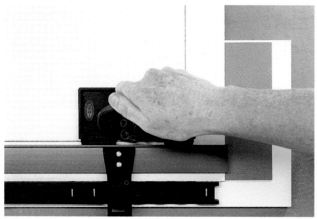

Each table-top mat cutter has its own unique cutting device and border-measuring system.

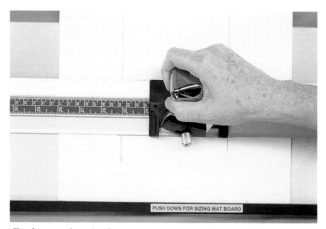

Each cutter has similar mat-penetration techniques that ensure clean corners.

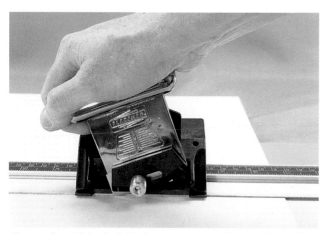

Cutters that fall in the hobbyist category include some devices that cut full-sized materials.

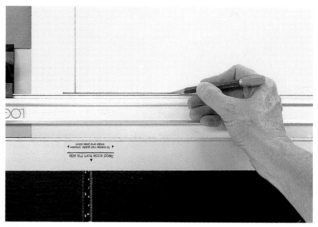

The mat-depth guides on these cutters make the measuring process faster and more accurate.

TABLE-TOP
CUTTERS

Many cutting heads also have indicator lines that help you determine the best entry and exit spot. This feature almost eliminates any overcuts or undercuts.

Cutting mats calls for some pressure and grip strength, but it doesn't require the power of a superhero. Blade penetration and even pressure are the keys to successful cuts. Some table-top cutters are designed to cut when you push the cutting head away from you, while others are designed to cut when you pull the cutter toward you. Both methods work well.

Indicator lines on the cutting heads help you recognize proper entry and exit locations.

Some table-top mat cutters are push cutters, some are pull cutters, and some cut in either direction.

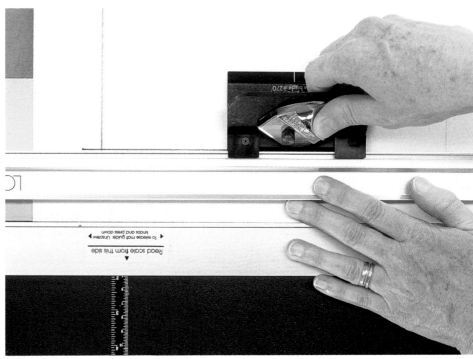

STRAIGHT-LINE MAT CUTTERS

Several straight-line mat cutters that cost less than $200 are available to home framers. Some of these tools have features and produce results that make them competitive with cutters designed for professionals. Each of these relatively inexpensive mat cutters has its own personality and offers something a little different. With practice, you can achieve high-quality mat cuts with any tool, but some cutters are easier to work with and cause less initial frustration. Try as many as you can in order to determine which cutter gives you the features you want for the amount you want to spend. Bear in mind that by cutting your own matting instead of having a framing business do it for you, you can save enough money to pay for a mat cutter in a short time.

ALTO 4501

With a retail price well below $100, this straight-line mat cutter is one of the least expensive mat cutters available anywhere. It is an outstanding cutter for the money. The cutting head is easy to grip and feels sure and accurate as you cut. The entire cutting blade and upright handle swing into the mat in order for you to complete a cut. This action is smooth and doesn't require great hand strength. Controlling the cutter is simple, and the cut indicator line makes starting and ending the cut foolproof. In addition, you can use the unit either right- or left-handed.

Changing the Alto 4501's blade isn't difficult either, even though you must remove a small blade-holding device to get to the blade. But this doesn't take long to accomplish, and the holding device fits easily back into its slot. To resume cutting, all you have to do is tighten the unit. All cuts are perfect 45-degree bevels and are push-cut.

The border-width measuring device has an ingenious peg-and-slot design. You can cut mat border widths up to $6^3/8$ inches in $^1/8$-inch increments. Because the Alto 4501 is open-ended, you can cut any size mat. The unit, whose base is 8×32 inches, is lightweight and easily transportable. The Alto 4501 comes with a great instruction book.

The Alto 4501 Cutter has a comfortable, upright grip handle. It glides along the edge of the mat-measuring device smoothly.

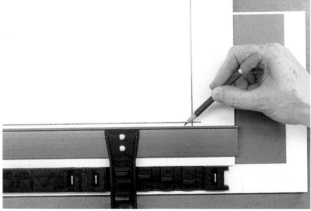

Alto's unique peg-and-step system measures borders in $^1/8$-inch increments up to $6^3/8$ inches.

TABLE-TOP CUTTERS

LOGAN COMPACT 301

This straight-line mat cutter is an especially well-designed unit that retails for under $100. The cutting head has a retractable blade. You can change the cutting blades quickly. All you have to do is loosen one small screw, replace the blade, and reset the screw. You are then ready to cut.

The Logan Compact 301's blade-entry design was smartly engineered. You guide the blade into the mat through a tiny slot in the cutting head. This aligns the blade and holds it in position, thereby preventing possible curves in the bevel. You simply apply adequate thumb pressure to push the blade through the mat and push-cut from the start line to the stop line. The cutting head, held in place by two guides, glides along a bar. All bevels are perfect 45-degree cuts. A straight cutter is available for reducing the size of large sheets of matting or foamboard. To do this, grip the cutter's upright handle and pull-cut through the material.

Any mat depth up to 5 inches is possible with the Logan Compact 301. The depth guide has a snap-to-release design that you can easily adjust in $^1/_{64}$-inch increments. The base is open-ended, so you can cut any size mat. The unit is lightweight and easy to transport. Included with the cutter is an instruction sheet for basic designs. The Logan Compact 301 is better suited for right-handed framers, but you can use it left-handed. The cutting head is designed to push-cut the mats. Here, you push the cutting head away from you. Gentle thumb pressure pushes the blade through the mat and holds the blade down as you push the cutting head away from the starting point.

FLETCHER-TERRY MATMATE 40" SYSTEM

This cutter has some wonderful features. The Fletcher-Terry MatMate 40" System was designed to cut full-sheet mats and backing materials. Despite the cutter's size, it is remarkably lightweight and easy to move around. As the unit's name suggests, the base can accommodate a 40-inch piece of mat board without needing to be repositioned during the cut. Start and stop indicator lines help you create perfect corners, and the blade/head configuration produces perfect bevels every time.

Also, this mat cutter has a drop-down ledge that quickly drops out of the way for sizing materials. You can use the cutting head either to push-cut or to pull-cut. The depth of the mat border can go as far as 7 inches. The unit has a well-designed blade-angle adjusting bracket that enables the same cutting head to cut both bevels and straight cuts. By simply attaching the specially engineered bracket under the bevel cutting head, you can make 90-degree-angle cuts.

Replacing the blade in the cutting head is the only weak point of this cutter. Because the blade position is adjustable, you must remove the entire blade, bracket, holding nut, and washer in order to change the cutting blade. Fortunately, however, this isn't difficult at all.

The price of this cutter is high, but its features are similar to those of a professional cutter. With a retail price of approximately $200, the Fletcher-Terry MatMate 40" cutter is a great buy. An instruction book is included with the unit.

LOGAN MAT-CUTTING KIT MODEL 525

This economical startup kit, which costs less than $75, contains everything you need to successfully cut beveled mats. You receive a mat knife for sizing your materials, a beveled mat cutter and cutting edge (Team System), a wonderful instruction guide, a sample mat board to practice on, and decorative, rub-on mat decorations.

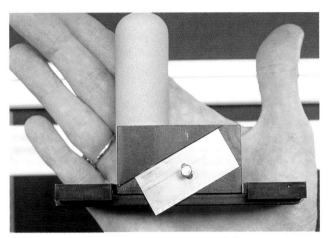

The Logan straight cutter operates on many of the company's mat-cutting devices.

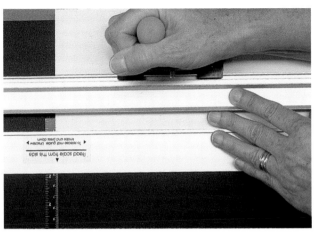

Grip the upright handle, and pull-cut. Because two cutting depths are possible, you can cut both matting and foamboard with the Logan Compact 301 and a straight-line cutter.

The Fletcher-Terry MatMate 40" System provides a special angle adaptor that converts a beveled cutter into a straight cutter.

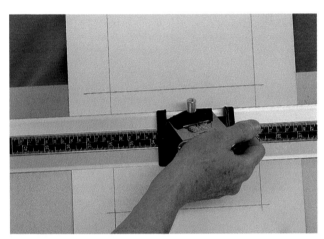

The Fletcher-Terry System can be used either right- or left-handed. The device has an ingenious design for cutting wide borders.

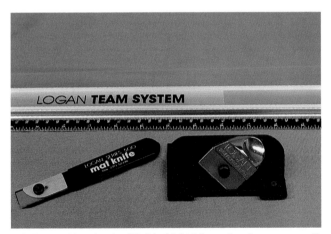

The Logan Mat-Cutting Kit Model 525 has a bevel cutter, as well as a cutting knife that you can use to reduce the size of full sheets of matting and backing. An instruction booklet and press-on decorative designs are also included in the kit.

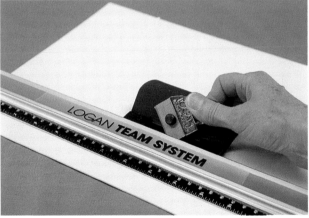

The cutter of the Logan Model 525 glides against the handheld cutting edge to yield great results for small and medium projects.

DECORATIVE CUTTERS

If creating spectacular, decorative windows interests you, you might want to consider some economical equipment additions. Whether used alone or with straight-line mat cutters, decorative mat cutters offer hundreds of combination cuts for personalized mat presentations. Circular windows provide an appealing way to display round images. Oval windows have long been a favorite for photographs because they spotlight the subject and crop out some of the background. You can achieve professional-looking results with any of the following special cutters at a cost of well under $100. Professional cutters can run more than $2,000.

ALTO CIRCLE CUTTER

This is one of the most uncomplicated circle cutters on the market. It uses a tack as a circle center-finder and has a retractable cutting head. Like Alto's straight-line cutter, the company's circle cutter uses common Dexter No. 3 blades in a flat bracket. The circumference measurer is pierced with holes in 1/8-inch increments. You press the head down, enabling the blade to easily cut through the mat and pivot around to complete the circle cut in one pass. This innocent-looking cutter isn't fancy, but it is remarkable. If it cut ovals, too, it would be unbelievable.

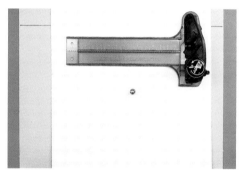

The Alto Circle Cutter makes circular shapes easily and efficiently.

Simply locate the center point, press in a positioning tack, depress the blade, and cut the circle.

Fancy combination cuts are simple when you use a straight-line cutter and a circle cutter. You can buy a couple of relatively inexpensive tools to produce top-quality decorative cuts that compare favorably with those made using professional equipment costing thousands.

The result: a perfect circle with no edge deviation.

This easy-to-use oval/circle cutter can cut either shape opening without any involved adjustments or tools. Four prongs on the bottom side of the base hold the unit in place. To center the base, first locate and mark a center cross. The cutting apparatus, which is outfitted with a depth lever to assist you in the proper cutting of the desired shapes, uses Dexter No. 3 blades. You must be careful when you do the mat-surface entry; afterward, cutting is a breeze. If ovals and circles are a part of your framing plans, you should take a close look at this unit.

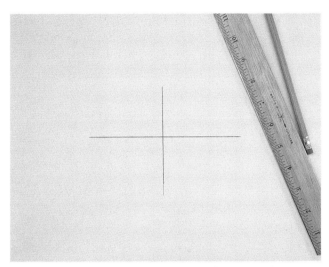

Start your oval cut by drawing a cross at the center of the mat.

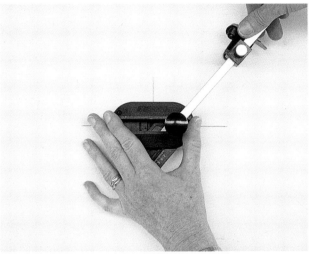

Place the cutting base on the cross, matching the indicator lines, and press the base prongs into the mat to hold the base in place. Then gently press and turn the cutter around the perimeter.

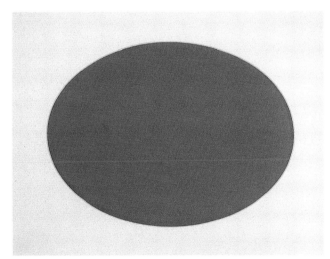

Flawless ovals are possible time after time when you use the Fletcher-Terry Oval/Circle Cutter.

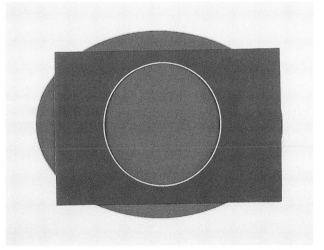

This cutter makes both ovals and circles in seconds. Switching from one shape to another doesn't require any additional tools.

TABLE-TOP CUTTERS

CLEARGROOVER

This small, hand-cast, acrylic designing tool is a mat carver's dream. The ClearGroover can cut any design you can draw in one of several depths of V grooves. Two Dexter No. 3 blades are aligned to cut simultaneously, thereby creating a perfect groove in the surface of a mat. With just one pass, both angled cuts are complete. This unit enables you to cut any kind of decoration on a mat, from thin, delicate lines to bold borders.

Using a straight edge with a ClearGroover produces professional-looking, straight-line V grooves around a mat window. Use the mat cutter's depth guide to assist you when making window V grooves. Make wild, show-stopping mats for your originals, or carve out a niche for your original mat creations. The retail price of the ClearGroover is around $40, a bargain when you consider the creative designing possible with it.

A gem of a decorating tool, the ClearGroover is amazing; it enables you to cut designs easily.

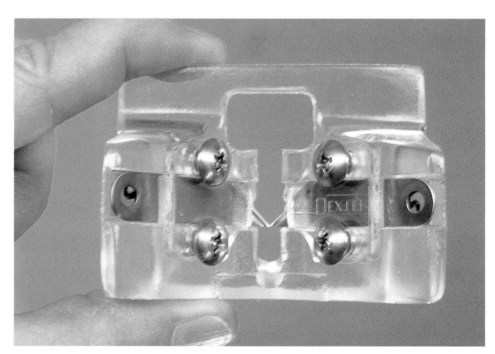

You can use a V groover to cut straight-line V grooves around windows or, working with it freehand, to create original designs effortlessly.

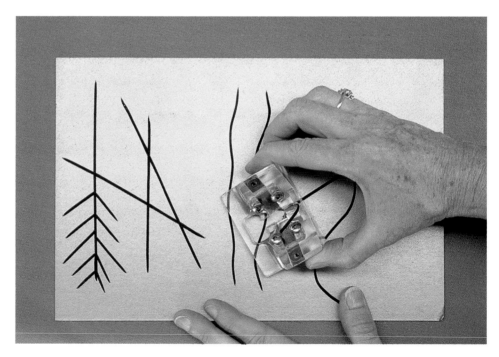

MAT-CUTTING PREPARATION

Cutting your own mats can be a rewarding experience, and you don't need to buy any expensive, specialized equipment to do it either. But you'll need some basic tools that you probably already have around your studio or work area. Before you get into the actual cutting, you should understand the basics of mat cutting. Whether you decide to learn the techniques of specialty presentation or stick to basic matting, you should try to keep the following points in mind.

Although mat cutting isn't a difficult procedure to master, it does require skill. You must practice in order to perfect the look you desire. Concentration during both the planning and the execution is vital. Proper measuring, while not at all hard, is the reason for most mat-cutting disappointments. You should always try to plan your project thoroughly from beginning to end before you cut any materials to size. Visualize the borders, and use your mind's eye to help you. There is an old carpenters' rule that always darts through my mind before I lay a knife blade or mat cutter to the surface of any material: Measure twice, and cut once. The length of time it takes to recheck your addition, subtraction, border allowances, multiple mat widths, weighted or wider bottom edge, and title window or any other part of the framing job is well worth whatever delay it represents in terms of completing the project. A single error in, for example, cutting the outside measurement could ruin a full sheet of mat board.

Invariably, this mishap will take place at a time when you are in a hurry getting ready for an exhibit, and the piece of matting you just ruined was your last. A number of unpleasant occurrences of this sort, and you may be tempted to toss your mat cutter out the window. Don't. Just remember to recheck your math, and everything will be fine.

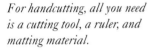

For handcutting, all you need is a cutting tool, a ruler, and matting material.

READY, SET, CUT!

The materials used to cut the window in a mat vary from a utility knife and a metal ruler to a mat cutter that costs more than $1,000. Realistically, amateur framers probably wouldn't be willing to invest in a professional cutter. In fact, I would never recommend that an artist, designer, or home decorator buy a professional cutter. This kind of equipment is built and priced for heavy use, such as cutting 100 mats per day for years. Obviously, this isn't what most framers require. Buy what is best suited to your needs. If you practice with handheld cutting knives, you can get them to yield perfectly cut mats.

So by spending as little as $3 to $5, you can buy the equipment you need to cut perfect mats that are completely acceptable in all artistic, decorating, and competition applications. For a little more money, you could purchase a safety ruler. This cutting aid is the safest way to hand-cut materials. The ledge protects your hand from a slip of the blade. Most such cutting edges have a slip-free base and make cutting much easier.

This is a good place for a brief pep talk about safety. Some of the most serious injuries occurring in framing shops are the result of carelessness with cutting blades. These cutting implements, whether they are mat-cutter razor blades, pointed blades with handles, utility knives, snap-blade cutters, or any other cutting apparatus, come out of the package with surgical sharpness. You can perform unexpected and unwanted surgery on yourself if you aren't careful.

Once you've done your mathematical calculations and double-checked them, your next step is to cut the mat board to frame size. Remember to work on a protected surface, and mark the lines on the backside of the mat. Transfer the frame-size measurements to the mat. Your cuts should be as accurate as possible because this shape provides the basis for window openings.

To draw the window shape on the mat, measure from the outside edges of the frame-sized mat, and mark the border widths. Border-measuring guides can help speed the process. Draw a box that indicates the size and shape of the window, crossing the lines at the corners. These crossed lines will provide the exact location at which you should start and stop your cuts.

If you begin your cuts outside this box, you'll end up with overcuts at the corners. If these cuts, which are difficult to hide, are severe enough, you'll have to redo the mat. Keep in mind, too, that any overcuts on hand-cut mats show badly. This is because the blade you use to cut such mats is usually a bit thicker and causes more trauma along the cut lines than a special mat-cutter blade.

When cutting museum mat board, always start with a fresh blade. Rag mats offer more resistance to the cutting edge, and the fibers dull the blade faster. It is wise to change the blade after any two cuts. The price of blades is low, and museum board is the most expensive mat board. It is far safer to replace the blade if you are in doubt. The only other difference between all other mat materials and museum board is thickness.

Safety cutting edges, like this FletcherEdge, effectively protect hands from slips of the knife.

The underside of some cutting edges has a nonslip strip to hold it in place.

You can use a border-measuring tool to speed up determining border sizes by hand.

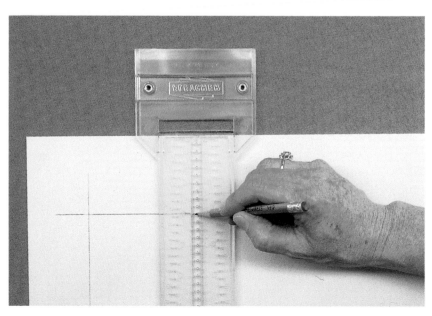

Grip the cutting knife firmly, and hold the blade straight along the side of your ruler. Even though this doesn't allow for a beveled edge, it is much easier than trying to maintain a steady angular cut. Start exactly at the point of intersection, and continue cutting with moderate to firm pressure. Keeping the pressure constant, cut to the next intersection, but not past it.

You might need to make two or more passes to cut through the mat material. As long as your blade retraces the preceding cut exactly, the cut will be clean and crisp. If the blade follows another path, the resulting cut will be ragged and won't look as good as it could. With a little practice, you'll soon master applying the correct pressure and angle that yield the exact cuts you desire.

The corners pose the biggest challenge. Because you might be somewhat apprehensive or tense when you start to cut, you might not cut the corners completely through. However, this problem is actually far more desirable than over-cutting them. To successfully cut corners, simply insert a mat-cutter blade or a safety razor blade into the cut line. Then work into rather than away from the corners. If the window doesn't fall out, check the corners and do additional cutting if necessary. Next, examine both the cut edges and the corners. Critique the angle of the cut and the crispness of the corners. If your first few attempts aren't perfect, try again.

This technique can be a bit difficult. You must hold the ruler with one hand and do the cutting with your other hand, all the time remembering to hold the knife upright. Despite this, you can learn to cut perfect mats with practice. As your skill level and interest demand more specialized framing looks, you'll need to buy a few pieces of equipment, beginning with a mat cutter. This equipment doesn't have to be expensive; many fine items are available in a hobbyist price range that yield professional results.

Another option is to work with one of the small, handheld cutters on the market, all of which do a fine job. These mat cutters are a step up from the ruler and cutting knife. They employ an angled blade that automatically controls the bevel cut. Although these bevel cutters are small and simple, they can cut beautiful mats. Again, you need a good metal ruler for the cutter to glide against. You mark and cut your borders from the backside exactly as you would with any mat cutting.

The major obstacle to cutting mats with a handheld bevel-cutting device is the same one that using a handheld knife produces. You must hold the ruler/guide securely against the mat, so that the cutter follows a straight and true path. In addition, seeing where some of these cutters are cutting can be hard. Fortunately, you can take advantage of a learning curve as you practice. The effort you put in is well worth it because the results can rival those you make with any bevel cutter.

Handheld cutting devices offer automatic beveled edges.

Controlling the cutting device and straight edge takes a bit of practice and patience.

Draw lines that resemble a box on the backside of the mat in preparation for cutting the window.

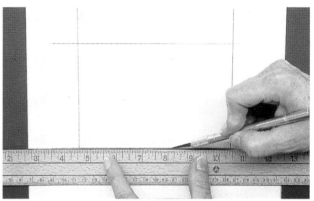

Cut through the mat several times. Make sure that each successive pass is in the path of the original score line.

Perfect corners are possible with little practice.

Straight-cut mats are as acceptable on artworks as beveled-cut mats.

CUTTING A SINGLE MAT

Mat cutting is actually a combination of several activities. Once you master cutting a single mat, you have all the skills needed to complete any matting project. Some mats might require a bit more measuring, marking, or cutting. Also, you might have to practice a little with the bevel-direction changes on some cuts. But this fine-tuning is simple once you get going.

Remember, the image measurement is what all subsequent dimension calculations are based on. You add the width of the mat borders to the image area in order to determine the frame size. After your calculations are complete, your next step, before you do anything else, is to cut all the materials you intend to use to the frame size.

To begin, draw cutting lines on the backside of the mat. Cut the window with a mat-cutting device. Inspect the cut edges of the window. If the mat is cut satisfactorily, continue with the framing process. If it isn't, you need to do a little more work.

Suppose that while inspecting the mat window, you discover a slight frayed or fuzzy look on the mat's colored surface. You can easily repair this condition by carefully "sanding" the surface with an emery board. Bear in mind, however, that there is a reason for the fraying; the most likely one is a dull or chipped mat-cutting blade. Changing the blade produces two results. First, the resistance of the mat against the blade will be reduced, thereby making the cutting process easier. Second, the window edge will be completely smooth, without any frays or burrs.

From an economic point of view, blades are far less costly than the mat board you're cutting, especially if you're using an exotic silk, a suede, or some other special surface finish. It makes good sense to change the blade if you have any doubt about its sharpness. Most mat cutters let you flip the blade, end over end. This gives you two sharp cutting tips on each blade. If one end chips or seems dull, simply remove and reverse the blade for a fresh, sharp edge.

Corners that aren't perfectly square or that seem to dip or hook are an indication of two possible problems happening at the start of your cut. Again, a dull blade that you push through the mat board might resist that penetration and bend slightly, thereby causing a hook. When you put in a fresh blade, the hooks will probably disappear. Pressing the blade through the mat too quickly with a downward rather than a rocking motion often produces a hook, too. Try to adjust your approach to each cut. As you press firmly against the blade-holding device, allow the blade to penetrate the mat with a gradual swing rather than a surge.

The Alto 4501 Cutter in use, cutting a single mat window.

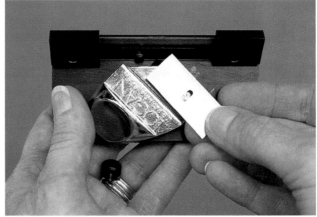

All straight cutters allow blades to be flipped end to end. This gives you two fresh, super-sharp cutting edges on every blade.

As you start to use your chosen mat-cutting equipment, you might need to recut along one of the sides of a window opening. When you use a mat-cutting device, the cutting blade often fails to align with the original cut. So the first pass cuts in one place, and the second pass cuts in another. This causes a thin sliver of mat board to appear along the beveled edge of the window opening. Filing it away might produce a satisfactory edge, but you'll most likely be unhappy with the result. The best way to fix this problem is to practice a bit more, and then train yourself to apply the proper pressure in order to cut through the mat in one pass.

Because museum mat board is just slightly thicker than all-rag or regular mat board, you might have to alter the blade-cutting depth a little in order to achieve a clean, one-pass cut. All mat cutters have such an adjustment. When you finish cutting museum matting, it is advisable to reset the cutter to the correct depth for regular mats. The slight increase needed for museum mat cutting could create hooks and curves on regular mats.

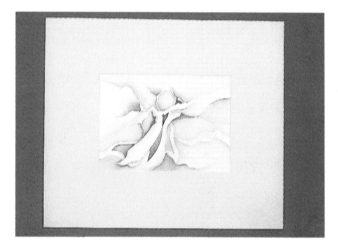

Left: You don't need superhuman strength to hold and guide a table-top cutter in order to cut out a perfect window.

Below: Untitled. June Adler. Watercolor with single mat. This floral study shows how simplicity can be quite complementary to a stylized image.

CUTTING A MAT WITH TWO WINDOWS

For some projects you'll want to mount two or more images within one mat. Double- or multiple-opening mats aren't difficult if you follow a simple plan. Imagine, for example, you want to cut a mat with two openings for two $5 \times 7^{1}/_{2}$-inch images. In addition to the border widths, you want a 1-inch separation between the two images.

To make the calculations simple and clear, sketch your proposed layout on graph paper. Use paper that is divided into even squares, each of which represents $^{1}/_{2}$ or $^{1}/_{4}$ inch. In the very center of the paper, mark the vertical center strip of matting that will be between the two images. To the right and left of this center division, measure the number of squares equal to the width of the photographs. Then draw lines to represent the edges of the windows. Be sure to remember the overlap required to hold the images in place. Do the same for the top and bottom of the two windows.

Next, around the two boxes you now have on the graph paper, decide on and mark the outside borders you want around the two windows. Check your calculations, and review the way your plan looks. Convert these figures to $^{1}/_{4}$-inch increments, and then calculate the outside dimensions of the mat. Transfer these measurements to the mat, and cut the outside measurement.

Lay the mat, color side down, on your work surface or in a mat-cutting device with a border-depth indicator. Mark the desired border all around the mat. Remove the mat from the depth guide, and measure by hand for the center division section. The easiest way to do this is to measure from the left outside edge toward the center of the mat first, and then from the right outside edge toward the center of the mat. Measuring from the outer edges of the mat in toward the center automatically indicates the two windows with a division between them. Then measure again to verify that you've drawn the lines correctly.

At this point, you repeat the technique you used to cut a single mat, making only one change. What makes double windows different is, of course, the division section between the two openings. Cut the three outside lines around each window first. Be sure to raise and lower your cutting blade when you come to the division section.

Keep the following rule in mind when you make the two center cuts: "If your cutting device is sitting on the window you want to cut, the bevel will be cut in the correct direction." So the cutting head should be on the area of the mat that will fall away after you make the cut, not on the division section between the two windows. If you accidentally cut with the cutting head on the division section rather than the window, the bevel will be reversed and you'll have to start again.

You can amplify these plans to include as many photographs, sketches, stamps, greeting cards, baseball cards, or other art objects as you wish. Remember to allow $^{1}/_{2}$ inch or more between the windows so that the finished collection doesn't look crowded. If you use graph paper each time, your success will be virtually guaranteed. If you're cutting windows for items of different sizes or in a special arrangement, remember that the lines you draw and cut from the backside will create windows in the opposite location when you turn the mat over. Keep this in mind when you make your initial plans.

If your collection consists of old photographs, perhaps heirloom photographs, you should have copies of them made before you begin your project. Mat and frame the copies, and store the originals in a safe place. This precautionary measure not only protects irreplaceable items from damage, but also enables you to have additional copies made for other family members or for friends. And when they see the results, they'll want you to frame the images for them, too!

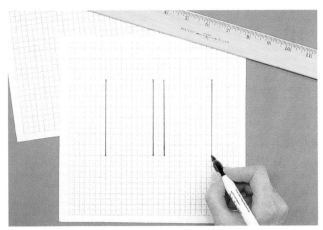

Plan the placement of your windows starting from the center of the page.

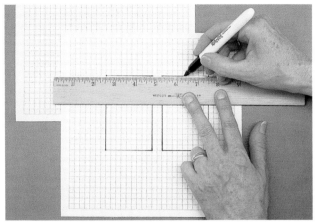

After you calculate the position of the openings, draw on the top and bottom of each window.

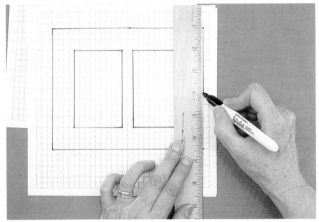

Add the border widths to these windows. The result is the finished size.

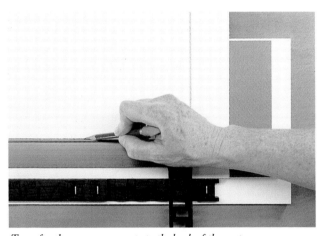

Transfer these measurements to the back of the mat.

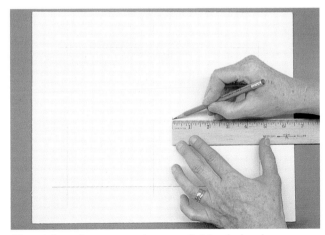

You might need to measure the center division by hand.

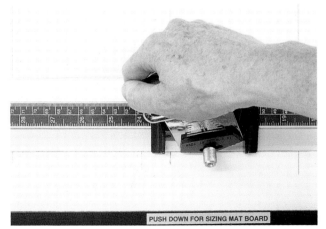

When cutting, whether by hand or with a mat cutter, remember to stop and restart your border cuts when you come to the center division.

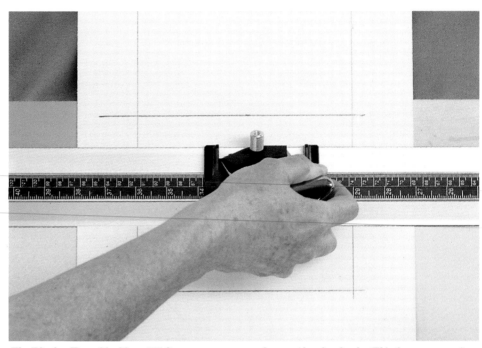

The Fletcher-Terry MatMate 40" System can cut extensive mat-border depths. This feature comes in handy for specialty cuts, such as a multiple-opening mat.

The result: a double-opening mat. With careful planning, you can cut any number of desired windows in a single mat.

An antique book illustration
and an accompanying poem
make a wonderful combination
in this single-mat/double-
window presentation. The
black-core mat enhances the
appearance of the double mat
by giving it definition around
the images.

"Artistamps" is another
example of two windows in
a single mat. Here, the title
of the rubber-stamp artwork
and the artist's name are
included in what is called
the title window. Artwork
courtesy of Beth Jacobs.

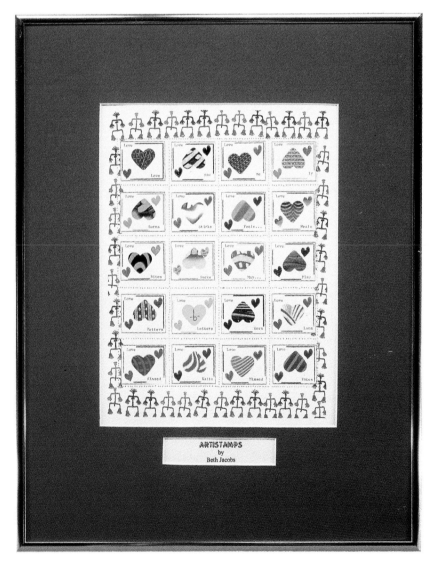

CUTTING A DOUBLE MAT

Cutting a single mat differs from cutting a double mat in only one way. With a double-mat project, when you cut the second mat, you're actually cutting two pieces of mat board that are attached. So treat them as one piece.

Begin your double mat by cutting the outside measurement of your top mat to the finished frame size. After cutting the outside perimeter, mark the window line at $1^3/4$ inches. This leaves $1/4$ inch for overlap. Then cut the mat window.

Next, place the top mat face down on your work surface, and put the fallout back into the window opening. All measuring and marking for both mats is based on the outside shape of the top mat. This is because you measure from the outside perimeter toward the mat's center. If there is a slight discrepancy in the shape of the mat, the window will echo that same discrepancy. In order for the top mat to dictate both window openings, it is necessary to reduce the dimensions of the bottom mat. Cut the bottom mat $1/2$ inch smaller in width and length than you did the top mat. This prevents any conflict in size between the two mats.

Glue or tape the face of the bottom mat to the backside of the top mat. You can join the mats several ways. You can use regular white glue, another adhesive of your choice, or double-faced tape. Double-sided tape holds well, doesn't require any drying time before you can continue, and is easy to use.

Place the double-sided tape on the backside of the top mat, $1/2$ inch outside the window, and then press the two mats together to bond them. Next, tape the fallout window of the top mat to the bottom mat. This supports the bottom mat and produces a cleanly cut window in the second mat. Once you join the two mats, treat them as one piece. After you mark cut lines at 2 inches on all sides, cut the window. When the window falls out and you turn the mat to face you, you'll see the result of a perfectly aligned double mat.

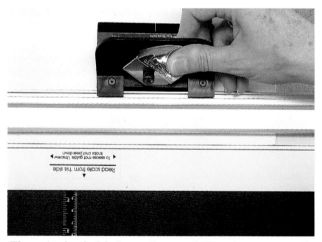

The cutting head of the Logan Compact 301 is quite accurate and easy to push.

Always reduce the size of the bottom mat of a double-mat assembly.

Attach the bottom mat to the top mat with strips of double-sided tape.

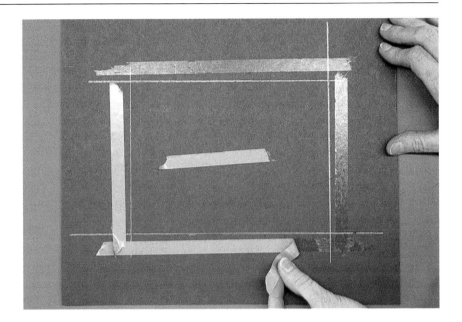

Once you join the top and bottom mats, treat them as one piece. Then cut the opening in the bottom mat.

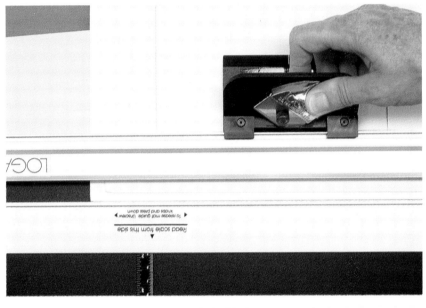

The result: a double mat with precise borders.

CUTTING A DOUBLE MAT

Professional framers often like to use a slightly wider mat-border area beneath the image. To help you achieve this look, set the depth guide at the width choice for the top and sides, and then mark those sides. Be sure to change the depth guide for a wider bottom border, and mark and cut this border. Next, reset the depth guide for the top and sides, and cut them. This saves a little time.

Finally, keep in mind that no rules govern color placement. But more double mats have light top coloration and contrasting or vivid bottom mats than dark top mats and light bottoms. Of course, the piece of art will dictate its own needs.

Here, the choice of a gold frame and a narrow, metallic bottom mat visually links the matting and the frame.

Subtle, natural colors and a warm-tone wooden frame accent this high-desert scene. The matting coordinates with its coloration, thereby making the transition from image to frame smooth.

GLAZING MATERIALS

Glazing materials are the coverings that protect artworks from dirt and other airborne contaminants in the environment. These products are divided into two groups, glass and plastics. Different types of glass are available for home framers. The two most commonly found kinds are clear and nonglare. And although glass breaks readily, it is actually quite durable. This characteristic, along with its ability to be cleaned easily, makes glass the most frequently used material for framing artworks.

Plastics, such as styrene and Plexiglas, are almost unbreakable, clear, and lighter in comparison to their glass counterparts. But their surfaces are fragile and scratch easily. Finally, specialty glazing materials, such as invisible glass, conservation glass, and UV Plexiglas, have more limited availability, but they offer many framing possibilities.

The matting selected for this photograph of a California coastline echoes the smoky tones in the image.

CLEAR GLASS

Framing professionals refer to ordinary glass as clear, window, and regular glass. Whatever you call it, this kind of glass is readily available, and you can have it cut to whatever size you need when you buy it. Clear glass is the least expensive, distortion-free glazing material you can purchase. It doesn't soften the image or cause loss of detail in the framed artwork. Clear glass varies in tint, but this slight coloration is seldom a factor in framing. The only exception is when super-white whites are part of the art. The primary function of clear glass is to protect a piece of art from the dirt and grime of everyday life, which it does well.

Clear glass does, however, have some negative aspects, such as its low UV-reflection property. Clear glass reflects only 46 percent of the UV light that attempts to attack the artwork underneath it. Some people consider the reflections often seen in clear glass objectionable. For example, the entire face of a piece of framed art can be too shiny to see when hung in bright locations.

When you get the glass home and are ready to begin working, you'll probably need to clean it. Simply spray a bit of household glass cleaner on one side of the glass, and wipe it with a paper towel. Repeat on the other side. Make sure that you remove all paper fibers before you begin your project.

When using clear glass as glazing on any piece of art, you can expect a bit of reflection. The amount of reflection is related to the amount of direct light that hits the spot where the art is hung. The more light, the more reflection.

NONGLARE GLASS

Nonglare glass is popular among framers because it has much less surface glare than clear glass. An acid-etching technique on the surface of clear glass is responsible for this glare reduction. You can purchase nonglare glass at most art-supply stores, hardware and building centers, and framing shops. The cost of nonglare glazing is approximately twice that of clear glass.

As you plan a project, keep in mind that the glare-free etched quality of nonglare glass softens some artwork. This loss of fine detail becomes more acute when you elevate the glass above the artwork via spacers or matting. A double mat (two thicknesses of matting) is the highest elevation possible before image clouding and extreme loss of detail occur.

Like clear glass, nonglare glass has a UV-reflection capability of 46 percent. But to its credit, nonglare glass enables you to hang art objects in rooms where a great deal of natural light floods in. And, like all other glazing materials, nonglare glass provides protection from dirt and grime. You clean nonglare glass the same way you clean clear glass.

This etching (also shown on page 91) is displayed under nonglare glass. Here, the reflection of the direct illumination is soft and barely visible.

CONSERVATION GLASS

This glazing material is unlike any other. A relative newcomer to the glazing arena, it affords art pieces the highest possible UV protection, approximately 98 percent. Conservation glass is made by a process in which a special UV-reflective coating is fused onto the surface of high-quality glass. This coating is itself clear and causes no loss of detail. Some tint occurs in the production of conservation glass because it is based on clear glass. Again, this tint is most noticeable on the whitest of whites. This glass comes in both clear and nonglare surfaces. It is available at custom-framing shops and some framing-supply centers and costs approximately 10 times the amount of clear glass.

If you decide to work with conservation glass, you should keep in mind the following two points. First, make sure that the coated side of the glass faces the artwork. Second, this coating is relatively fragile and scratches easily, so you should clean the treated side with a damp, soft cloth using side-to-side strokes. Clean the coated side first, and then lay it over the completed artwork "sandwich." Next, clean the outside of the glass. No special handling is required for the outside because it isn't coated.

These side-by-side comparison shots show the difference between clear and nonglare conservation glass. The reflections are quite similar to those of regular glass and nonglare glass, but you can't see the UV-blocking coatings that enable conservation glass to effectively protect art.

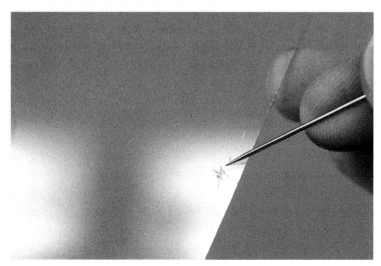

This simple test is used to determine the coated side of conservation glass. The protective coating scratches easily, but the plain side doesn't. Always have the coated side face the artwork; let the untreated surface face the outside.

INVISIBLE GLASS

The newest glazing material on the market is what might be called a miracle product. This revolutionary glass is virtually invisible when placed over an artwork. A patented acid-etching technique gives the surface a nonglare appearance that is especially soft. No reflections occur on the surface, and no distortion of detail occurs in the artwork. These two qualities make invisible glass ideal for framing needlework and highly detailed renderings.

But you do have to take into account the limited UV protection invisible glass provides, which is approximately the same as that of both clear and nonglare glass. The best way to clean invisible glass is to use the special cleaner designed for it, which is available at the point of purchase. A somewhat successful alternative is to use rubbing alcohol; it removes fingerprints from the glass's surface.

Truly a product that must be seen to be appreciated, invisible glass is worth its high cost for some applications. Its price is about 12 times that of clear glass. This very special glazing material is available only at high-end, leading-edge framing shops or framing-supply centers.

When handling invisible glass during the framing process, you should wear cotton gloves or grip the glass surface with soft material. Cleaning oil from your fingers off the etched surface can be difficult. Special cleaners are available wherever you buy invisible glass.

PLEXIGLAS

Plexiglas, which is actually a clear, acrylic sheet, has several wonderful qualities that make it different from any other glazing material that protects artwork. Plexiglas is lightweight and flexible, which are important features when a piece of art is large. And Plexiglas is almost unbreakable, so it is great for game rooms and children's rooms. Because the acrylic sheeting is perfectly clear—and is the only glazing material that is—it is ideal for black-and-white photography. It enables the whites to be really white. Remember to elevate the Plexiglas off the surface of the photographs so no adhesion occurs.

You shouldn't ignore the weight factor, especially when you plan to frame an oversized artwork. The weight of acrylic sheeting is about half that of glass-type materials. And the high flexibility of acrylic sheeting is quite helpful in terms of transporting and hanging large pieces of art. Unlike glass, Plexiglas can withstand a great deal of surface pressure during hanging and cleaning, and even more flexing during transport.

Plexiglas is reasonably economical, which is important when you work with large pieces. The bigger the artwork, the more glazing material you need and the higher the expense of the project. The sheets are available in both clear and nonglare surfaces. One type of Plexiglas has a UV-reflection property that rivals that of conservation glass.

The only real drawback to acrylic sheeting is the difficulty in keeping the surface scratch-free. When cleaning Plexiglas, spray the surface with a suitable cleaner; special Plexiglas cleaners help reduce the static on the surface. Spray or douse a soft paper towel with the cleaner, and wipe in a side-to-side motion. Lightly draw the toweling across the surface without circular motion and excessive pressure. Continue to pick up the moisture this way until the surface seems dry. Always remember to dampen the crushed paper toweling before rubbing it on the fragile surface. Polishes that help remove light surface scratches are available, but they don't come with guarantees that they won't add to the problem rather than fix it. Vacuum-cleaner attachments are too stiff and will undoubtedly scratch the Plexiglas.

The prices for clear and nonglare acrylic sheeting are roughly five times the price of clear glass. UV-reflective acrylic sheeting costs about 8 to 10 times as much as clear glass. A new scratch-resistant UV acrylic sheeting is available at double the price of regular acrylic sheeting. You can buy Plexiglas at many art-supply centers and frame shops, as well as at some hardware and building centers.

Peel the slightly tacky backing off the Plexiglas right before you fit the artwork into the frame. Removing this protective covering should be the last step you make before you close the work.

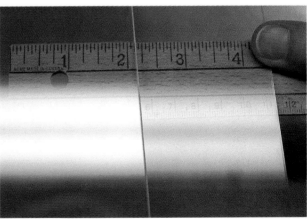

This side-by-side comparison shot of clear Plexiglas (left) and regular clear glass (right) shows that their reflective qualities are similar.

STYRENE

At the bottom of the list in visual quality is styrene, a thin, lightweight glazing material. Styrene is used extensively in the sign-making industry as a clear, protective surface. Styrene is quite easy to cut and is available at most building-supply centers and hardware stores. Some art-supply centers and framing suppliers carry styrene in precut sizes.

If you are an artist and carry your work around the show circuit, styrene might be of real value to you in your framing. It is lightweight and virtually unbreakable, just like acrylic sheeting. Styrene has a protective plastic cover that you have to peel away right before you place it on artwork. But if a piece of styrene does somehow get damaged, replacing it doesn't require a large investment. You can use styrene on any artwork and in any decorating situation. Keep in mind, though, that styrene is considered a lesser-quality product than other glazing materials. And although it produces little distortion, it isn't as clear as Plexiglas.

If customer resistance is a worry, offer to trade the styrene for clear glass or other material at no charge to the customer. The fact that you aren't carrying and breaking glass or carrying and destroying acrylic sheeting more than makes up for the expense that you might incur. In addition, such service makes clients feel special and appreciated.

The clear, plastic, protective covering on styrene is easier to peel away than the covering on Plexiglas. The removal of either coating does, however, charge the surface with static electricity. This static, in turn, draws in dust and debris from the work area.

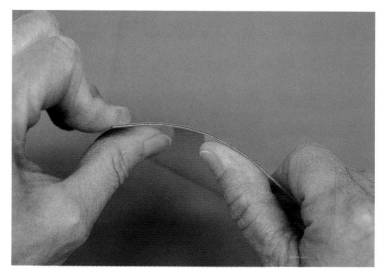

Because styrene is so thin, it is quite pliable and easy to cut. Lightly score the surface with a utility knife, and snap along the line to evenly break the material to the desired size.

WORKING WITH GLAZING MATERIALS

Because glass is dangerous, you should be alert and be safety conscious when you work with it. Never use or move glass sheets around children or pets. When you transport large sheets of glass, wear gloves to protect your hands. Grip the top edge firmly, and lift the glass without flexing it. Avoid thermal shock to the glass and possible in-hand shattering by storing and working with it in temperature-controlled areas.

Glass stored at the ambient temperature of a typically warm warehouse microscopically expands. When you bring this glass into a cool, possibly air-conditioned work area, the colder air shocks the glass, causing it to contract and perhaps shatter the glass into splinters. The reverse—moving glass from a cool space into a warm one—can also shatter the glass. Try to store and use glass at the same temperature in order to eliminate the chance of thermal shock.

You can cut glass on any clean, flat surface that is covered with something to slightly pad it. Corrugated cardboard and low-pile carpet make good surface coverings. Corrugated board is especially good because you can draw an alignment line on it; this will help you accurately measure the glass.

Fletcher-Terry offers two glass-cutting tools. One is a traditional tool with a cutting wheel at one end and a tapping ball at the other. This implement is easy to grip and provides a clean cut. The other glass cutter has a special feature that provides the cutting wheel with continuous lubrication. This wick-and-oil reservoir automatically dispenses a small amount of oil with each revolution of the cutting wheel. This lubrication can significantly lengthen the life of the cutting edge. The shank of the cutter is a little bigger and longer, which is an advantage because these extra dimensions make the cutter easy to hold. Both Fletcher-Terry cutters are available wherever matting supplies are sold.

This is a basic glass-cutting tool. More sophisticated models have a wick that continuously lubricates the cutting wheel.

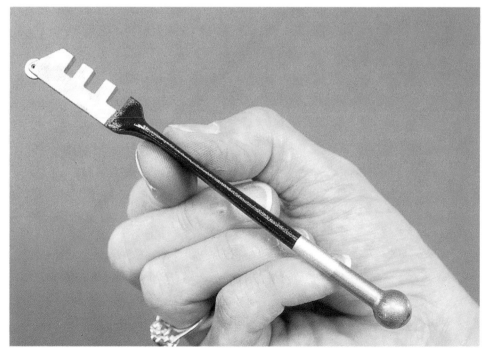

To size your glass, simply draw a vertical line, lay the glass over the line, and slide the glass to the right or left of the line to the desired dimension. Using a metal ruler as a guide, score the glass down the vertical line drawn on the work surface. Never rescore the cut line because this will dull the cutting wheel. After scoring, lightly tap the glass from the underside with the ball end of the hand cutter along the entire length of the score. Then carefully lay the glass on a table or workbench with the score line exactly above the edge of this work surface. Grip the overhang, and push with authority. Moderate pressure is all it takes to snap the glass right down the score line.

To cut circles or ovals out of glass, first score the glass in the desired shape. Remember to avoid rescoring over a previous cut. Next, score lines from the defined shape to the edge of the glass. The pattern should resemble the look of flower petals around a flower center. Lightly tap from the backside around the central shape first, and then along each of the score lines that divide the waste glass around the center. If tapping doesn't release the desired shape, gently break away each of the outer waste sections in order to reveal the center.

Initially, it is completely reasonable to purchase your glass precut to size at your local hardware store, building-supply center, or art-supply or craft store. In fact, until you begin to frame in quantity, buying glass this way is smart. What motivates most framers to cut glass is needing to size a piece of glass that they have on hand. Most low-volume framers find it more cost-effective and convenient to buy pieces cut to size rather than deal with the storage, moving, cutting, and disposal of glass scrap.

For safety and accuracy in cutting glass, you should establish an alignment line to help you measure.

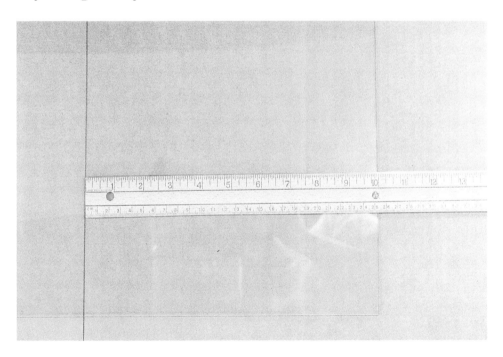

Once you place the glass over the alignment line, measure to the desired size, place a ruler along the line, and score the glass with a glass cutter.

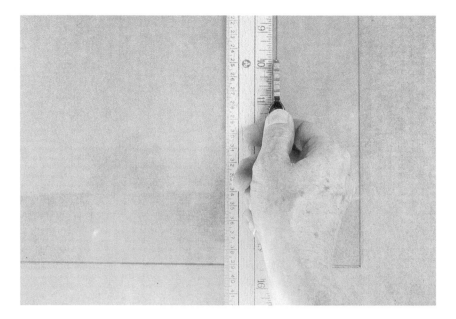

Tap the underside of the scored glass with the ball end of the cutter.

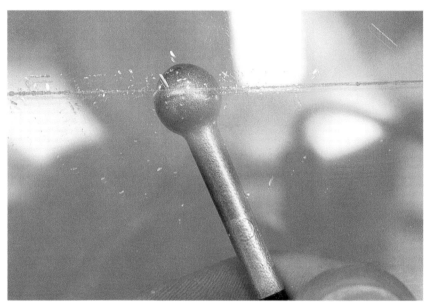

When you crisply press down against a piece of glass, a clean break will occur along the score line. Hold the art side of the glass with one hand, and sharply lunge against the trimmed waste piece. Never allow the glass to slide against your hand.

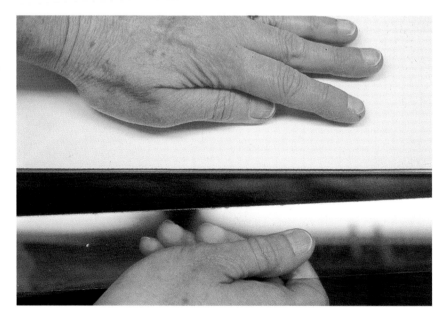

WORKING WITH GLAZING MATERIALS

Two other glazing materials, Plexiglas and styrene, are easy to cut and pose no danger to children or pets (or you) when stored in the home. To successfully cut Plexiglas, you must repeatedly score a line until you've penetrated at least $1/3$ of the way through it. You can use one of the special hand tools designed for cutting acrylic sheeting. When the scoring reaches the recommended depth, slide the piece to the edge of your worktable. Then with a brisk lunge, press against the scrap that is hanging over the side. The Plexiglas should snap right down the score line. Don't remove the protective paper covering before the piece is the exact size you want. In fact, I wait to peel it off until I am ready to put the package together and into a frame. The static charge created when you pull off this covering is quite strong and attracts every piece of debris and lint on the work surface. So, it is wise to wait until the last possible second to remove the covering.

You can use the same scoring-and-breaking technique with styrene. But because this glazing material is much thinner than Plexiglas, making just two passes along a score line is usually sufficient to facilitate breaking. As with acrylic sheeting, remove the protective plastic covering right before you are about to place the art assembly in the frame. Working with glass is simple as long as you practice basic safety procedures.

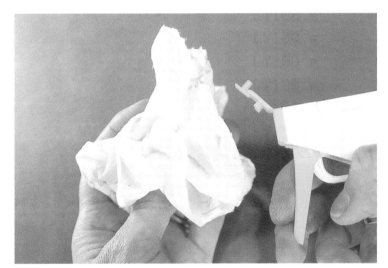

When cleaning any plastic glazing material, begin by wetting the toweling or soft cloth and lightly misting the surface to be cleaned. The two wet surfaces help prevent scratching. Dry material against Plexiglas and styrene will damage them.

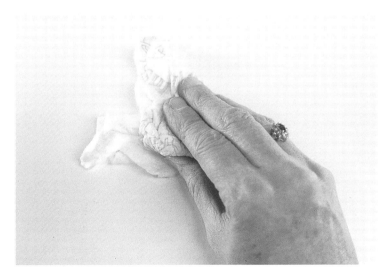

After wetting the surface of the Plexiglas or styrene with a wet cleaning cloth or paper, use a gentle, side-to-side motion to lift off any debris.

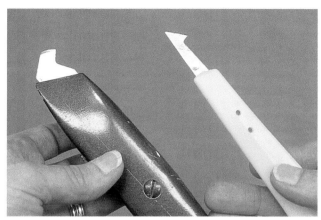

Plexiglas and styrene should be scored with a special tool.

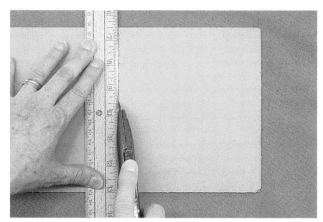

Draw the size desired on the protective covering, and then score the lines.

With some of the wrapper pulled away, you can see a visible score line. This is needed for a clean break.

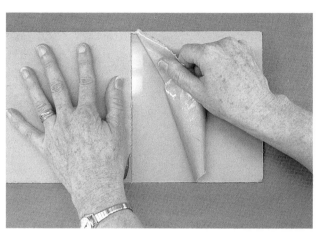

Remove the protective wrapper right before you place the artwork in the frame.

This side-by-side comparison of Plexiglas (right) and what is called clear glass (left) reveals that the Plexiglas is actually free of tint while the glass shows color.

CHAPTER 6

FRAMING

Most people, including artists, designers, and decorators, decide to frame their artwork collection for two primary reasons. The first is economy. Simply by gathering the materials and putting them together yourself, you can reduce the cost of custom framing by 30 to 40 percent, perhaps even more. You can seek out bargain frames, buy precut mats and glass, and put the entire package together. This can save you quite a bit of money. When professional framers gather this material for you, you pay their professional rates.

The second reason why people get involved in framing their artwork collection is for the pure fun of it. Selecting the mats, special touches, and frames for art pieces can be as rewarding as creating or collecting the artwork to begin with. The sense of accomplishment you experience when assembling the materials you've chosen is fulfilling. Many artists feel, and correctly so, that mounting, matting, and framing are simply extensions of the original creative process.

Framing stretched canvas is a fast, easy process. For "Under the Influence," an acrylic on canvas, I constructed the frame around the artwork and attached a wire.

ACHIEVING PROFESSIONAL RESULTS

If you've already tried framing and realized the benefits of doing your own work but you don't feel confident in your ability to complete some of the steps, let someone else do these tasks for you. For example, you can buy and cut the backing, complete a conservation mounting of an original artwork, buy precut glass, find a frame, and let a professional framer cut a special mat. This approach can easily save you between 25 and 30 percent of the cost of having the professional do all the work.

But keep in mind that professional framers are better equipped to do some specific projects than independent framers, who would have difficulty in completing them. For example, mounting large-scale maps and posters, as well as other oversized items, is the professionals' specialty. It is always wise to solicit an expert's help for any task that is beyond your ability.

As you begin to frame more frequently, you'll gather experience and develop confidence. You'll also want to buy some labor- and timesaving equipment. But before you spend a penny, you should examine the extent of your involvement in framing artworks, your own or others'. If you're going to frame just a few pieces of art a year, you won't need to get any additional equipment. If, however, you plan to derive a second income from framing, you'll need to buy some equipment.

The first such purchase is usually a table-top mat cutter. As mentioned earlier, for less than $200, you can buy one of several models designed for amateurs. Most of the cutters are efficient, compact, lightweight, and portable. A few hand tools and moderately priced specialty tools for framing can also save you time, energy, and frustration. But you probably already have what you really need around your house or studio.

In time and with practice, you may start to consider yourself a semiprofessional framer. At this point, upgrading your mat cutter is a good idea. A heavy-duty cutter, designed with features to streamline production and aid in sizing materials, could save you enough time and labor to justify the expense and, eventually, pay for itself.

"Ballerina." Lois Blackburn. Oil on canvas. This piece of art has a museum quality because the formality of the frame coordinates so well with the imagery.

READY-MADE FRAMES

For people who enjoy instant gratification, ready-made frames are a way for them to plan a framed artwork and achieve the look they want quickly. Ready-made frames are available in the same moldings that custom shops use and that are available through catalog framing suppliers. Major wholesale manufacturers of molding sell their stock to companies that sell ready-made frames to the mass market. These firms then make the most popular colors, textures, and finishes available in ready-made sizes. All of this means that you can easily coordinate the style of an artwork with a large number of current, good-quality, ready-made frames made from leading-edge molding stock.

One benefit of using ready-made wooden frames is that you don't need one single piece of exotic equipment because you have no frame building to do. The only item you need is a small hammer to place thin nails that hold the work in the frame. You don't need clamps, corner vises, glue, a miter box, or a saw. Another advantage to ready-made frames is that they can be quite affordable.

You can use a ready-made frame with any artwork. Many ready-made frames come complete with backing materials and glass. So all you have to do is loosen the closure apparatus, remove the backing, clean the glass, slip the glass and piece of art into place, and close the back. This is an oversimplification of the process, but it gives you a general idea of how easy it can be.

You can purchase basic frames in widths that fit the size of a piece of art for little more than metal-framing kits cost. However, your artwork might be more effectively exhibited in ornate frames. You can find these at large, warehouse-like framing centers for great low prices. Some discount art-supply stores and catalog framing suppliers usually carry a limited but dynamic selection of fancy, baroque-style, carved, frames. This type of molding gives a museum look to an art piece and often commands a much higher selling price. Remember this if you decide to market your works.

A real boon to occasional framers is the selection of custom-cut moldings available from catalog-order houses. These companies cut moldings to any size you desire. They send the frames to you either already joined or, in some cases, with a thumbnail slot routed into the end of each stick of molding. You simply have to apply adhesive to the mitered edges of the frame, and use a hammer to tap in a special corner piece that holds the parts of the frame together. These frames, which are easy to assemble, enable you to add a touch of originality to your framing projects.

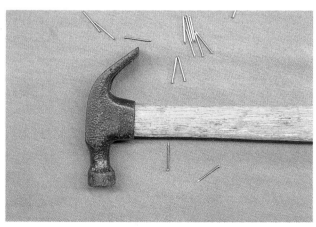

The only tools you need to fit a wooden frame are a hammer and long, thin brads.

With ready-made frames, framing is as simple as open, insert, and close.

"Frog." Alice Bertling. Mixed water media. The richness of this woodsy, forest-toned matting and ready-made wooden frame gives this quick study a simple yet cohesive presentation.

Ready-made wooden frames come in hundreds of styles. Carefully coordinating and artwork and framing materials is the key to success. The contemporary frame I selected for my acrylic monotype, made with mixed drawing materials, is a perfect complement.

METAL-MOLDING KITS

Metal kits provide framers with another opportunity for near instant gratification. All frame parts, hardware to join the frame, and special hangers are included in the kits. All that artists or decorators have to do is acquire a backing material and glass before they can begin framing. Metal frames have many great qualities, but amateur framers probably consider the most important ones to be availability and price. You can locate metal-molding kits at any art-supply store, discount art-products store, and almost every catalog framing supplier—in other words, just about anywhere. And the price of extruded aluminum molding is quite low. This type of molding is manufactured in a cookie-press fashion. Here, the aluminum is pressed through a die or design, and long lengths of molding are made quickly. The ease of this process contributes to the relatively inexpensive price.

You have a huge variety of colors and profiles to choose from. In fact, you could frame every piece in your home in metal molding and still have dozens of options remaining. Metal moldings come in colors and styles that are ideal for everything from works of art on paper to thick shadowbox displays.

Metal frames are strong, and, once assembled around an artwork sandwich, have an integrity that is unrivaled. This makes them a great choice for public exhibitions and show events. Furthermore, the metal frames themselves don't waste space, are easy to wrap and transport, and can withstand the rigors of the show circuit.

Assembling metal frames is quick and easy. Once you bring the corners together, simply use a flat-blade screwdriver to tighten the corner hardware, all of which is included in the kit. (If you order metal framing from catalog sources, you can order the necessary hardware at a low price simultaneously.) Join a long side and two short sides to form a squarish U shape. If double-corner hardware is provided in the kit, use the flat piece beneath the screw-on L piece. Then attach the last four pieces of hardware to the fourth piece of frame molding.

Metal frames come in dozens of profiles, textures, colors, and finishes. They represent one of the most versatile collections of moldings on the market. Some are available in kits that include all the required hardware. With glass and backing, you can frame artworks quickly and inexpensively.

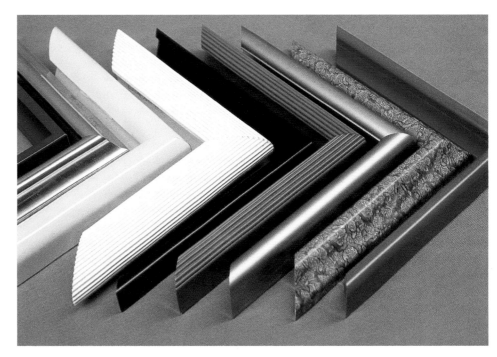

Two beneficial characteristics of metal moldings are their integrity and strength. Double corner brackets are screwed in place, and hold the unit with remarkable power.

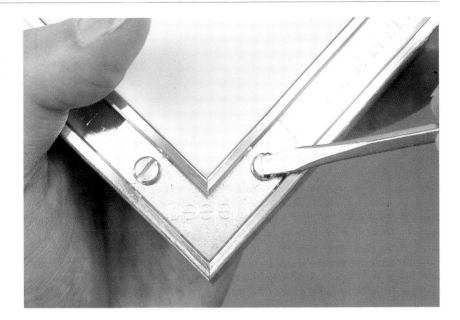

Join three sides of molding, insert the artwork sandwich, and then attach the fourth section.

Place the blank bracket in the hardware channel beneath the screw-on bracket. They work in tandem.

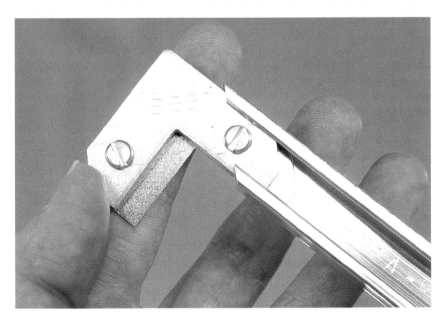

Next, slide the artwork into the U shape, and attach the fourth section of the frame. You actually construct the frame around the art sandwich. Attach the wire hangers. Two types of hangers are available: screw-on or snap-in. Put the wire on by first passing through the wire hangers twice. This provides additional strength for heavy artwork, but it is a good habit to develop for all framing projects. Tension on the wire should be relaxed enough so that a flattened fist can slide under the wire. Then twist the tails of the hanging wire at least six times, wrapping them close together and as near to the hanger as possible.

Spring clips, which are the slightly bowed metal bars included with the other hardware, hold the sandwich together in the proper place in the frame. They secure the contents of the frame snugly, so no shifting or rattling occurs. To install the spring clips, carefully slide them below the hardware channel until they are completely under the hardware edge. Begin with one end of the clip, and then swing the entire bar under the edge of the frame.

Once you've gotten the hardware in place and attached the wire, you don't need to do any additional finishing. All that remains is to put small rubber bumpers at the lower corners; these bumpers protect the wall and help keep the picture straight. Instructions are always provided for first-time framers, but after you've joined a metal molding, the technique is with you forever. It is that easy!

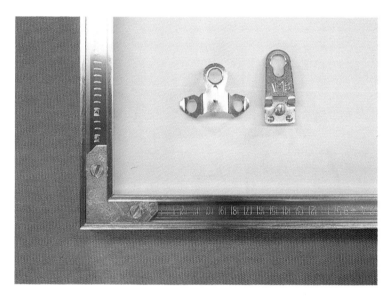

When selecting hardware, you have two common styles to consider: snap-in (left) and screw-on (right).

After you install the artwork in the frame, screw the wire holders into the hardware channel.

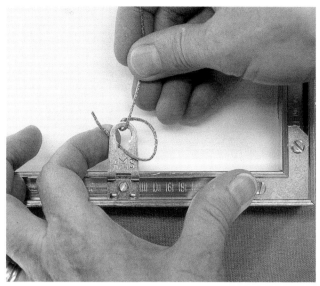

Attach the wire with a double pass through the wire hole.

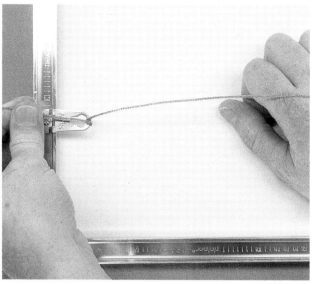

Tension on the wire is correct when you can pass your flattened fist under it.

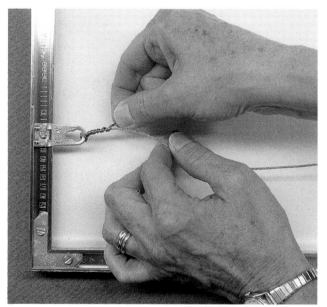

Wrap the tails of the wire as closely together and as close to the double pass through the wire hole as possible.

Spring clips hold the artwork unit in place, preventing shifting and rattling.

Matching the tones of the elements in a photograph with framing color choices and an off-center mat window can transform a pleasant artwork into a smashing one. This was the approach I took for my photograph entitled "Backyard Harvest."

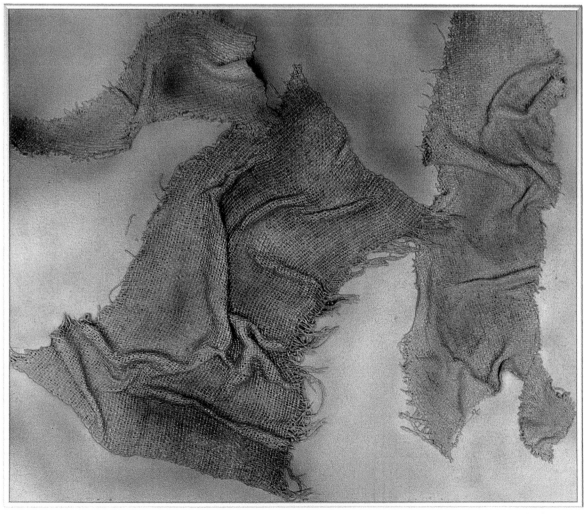

For "Tip of Texas," a rigid, handwoven fabric with acrylics, I decided to use the acrylics for both protection and coloration. I wanted to display this three-dimensional piece without glass.

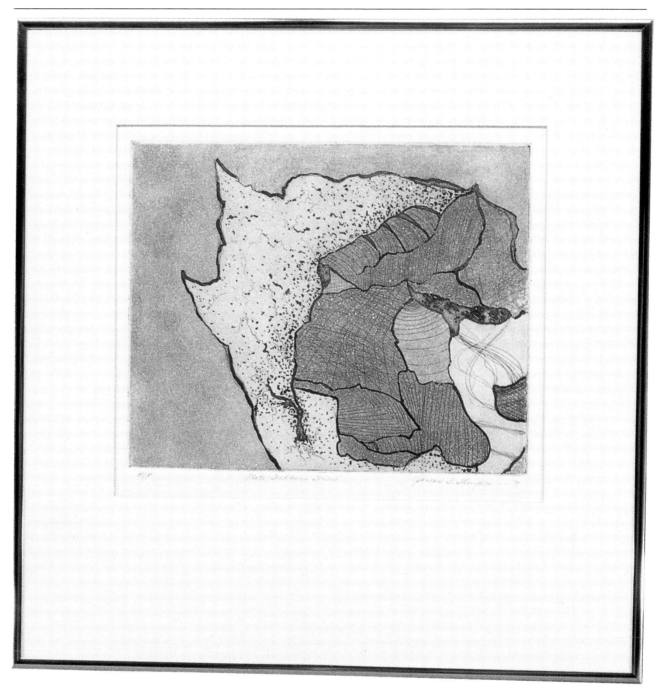

Gold and silver metal moldings are the most popular because they are so versatile. Warm tones are best suited to gold frames, and cool tones look best in silver frames. For "Plate Tectonics," an etching I made using sepia ink and a single, white, rag mat, I decided on a gold metal molding to enhance the warm colors in the piece.

MAKING BASIC WOODEN FRAMES

In the interest of economy, ease of construction, and overall simplicity, you can make one type of wooden frame for stretched canvas with little equipment. Lattice-strip frames marginally meet the requirements for displaying a work for a juried or a public exhibition. Nevertheless, they can look great with contemporary art. Because the frames are so thin, they don't interfere with the artwork or draw attention to themselves. The frames are composed of thin lattice strips of wood that are about 1/4-inch thick and come in various widths.

You don't have to miter the corners, so you can use any type of saw to cut the strips to the desired lengths. With care, you can actually use a sharp utility knife to cut through the lattice wood. Simply repeatedly score where you want to cut the piece. Once you've cut it, sand the edges and continue. If you use a saw, cut the strips to surround the stretcher bar. Remember, two lengths of the lattice must be the exact lengths of the canvas, and two must be longer. The amount of extra length is determined by the width of the lattice.

After cutting the wood, you can either paint the strips to coordinate with the piece art or leave them natural. To seal the surface, you might choose to coat it with an acrylic painting medium, but this isn't necessary. Attach the strips to the stretcher bars with small brads, or headless nails, that are about 3/4- to 1-inch long. Nail the lattice strip directly to the canvas stretcher bar. This requires only a nail at each end of the strip and perhaps one or two spaced along the length of the strip.

You can also make simple frames that are well suited to art on paper and illustration board, as well as stretched canvas. Artworks without structure (stretcher bars) need both support all around their perimeter and a frame that provides a channel to hold them in place from the backside. This channel is called a rabbet. It is possible to find suitable unfinished moldings with rabbets at lumberyards, and hardware and building centers. Some cabinet-making materials, corner moldings, door-casing moldings, decorative stained moldings, and raw-wood moldings are appropriate for picture frames.

You need some special tools and equipment to miter and join wooden molding. In order to cut the molding to the desired lengths, you must use a miter box and a saw. The miter box can be a simple wooden or plastic device with preset cutting angles. Some inexpensive mitering devices have blade guides, thereby making them a bit more accurate than those without guides. For mitering your molding, you'll usually want a wide-blade saw that doesn't taper at the end. This helps you keep even pressure and the required angle to cut a perfect 45-degree corner. Be aware, however, that holding the molding, miter box, and saw all at the same time can be a challenge.

Begin by determining the length of molding you need. Remember to add 1/16 inch to allow for the placement of the artwork sandwich. Put the molding in the miter box, and keep a strong grip on the molding throughout the process. Slowly work the saw through the thickness of the molding, without rocking or any other movement. Then draw the saw toward you gently to set the cut. Progress through the molding in a back-and-forth motion. Be especially careful as you make your last few passes through the wood. Splintering can occur and possibly damage the look of the completed frame. You need a smooth cut along that angle for a correct join at the corners. Using small C clamps can help hold the wood in position.

Once you've cut all four pieces of molding, lightly sand any irregularities from the cut edges. You might want to stain the wood or paint it an appropriate color for your project. Water-based stains and paints are the safest to use and dry fastest. Color all four sticks of molding before joining them. Then when the staining is completely dry, continue building your frame.

Nail the strips directly to the edges of the stretcher bars.

The completed lattice frame is a simple, inexpensive project.

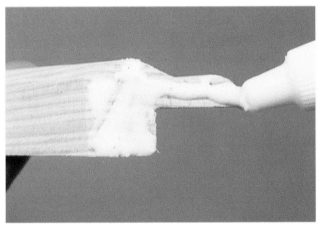
When working with a wooden frame, you set the art into a channel called the rabbet.

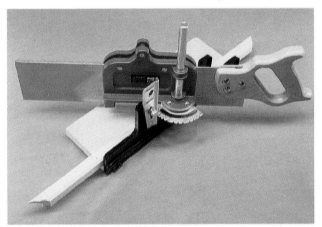
This unit is outfitted with cutting guides.

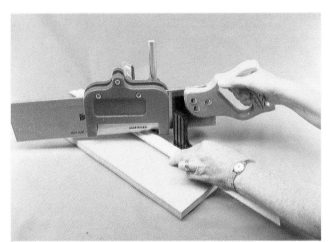
You must have a firm grip on the molding to prevent it from slipping during the cutting process.

After sawing the molding, sand away any tiny splinters.

Joining corners isn't difficult if you have corner clamps. These are available at hardware and building centers and come in a variety of styles. One type permits you to simultaneously join all four corners of the frame. The Merle clamp is an example. Most styles, however, clamp one corner at a time. Both types of clamps do a great job.

Lightly apply glue to both ends of the two lengths of molding that you're joining. You should use the type of glue specifically recommended for joining wood to wood. It is also advisable to use a small brad at each corner in order to help hold the frame together. The glue is actually what keeps the frame together; the nail is simply insurance.

If possible, you should do any nailing needed with the corner bracket in place. The shock of each tap of a hammer could break the adhesive apart and cause the corner to lose its bond. This, in turn, would force you to redo the corner. If you find that a corner has popped lose during the completion of your framing and that only the nail is holding the corner together, you can reglue that corner.

Using a syringe, available from your pharmacist, is an excellent way to dispense a bit of glue into a tiny opening between two pieces of the frame. Syringes with large orifice needles are the easiest to work with because the glue flows readily from their tips. Fill the barrel of the syringe with a teaspoonful or less of glue, apply where needed, clamp the corner, and then wash the barrel to remove the glue before it hardens. If the needle's orifice dries with glue in it, snip off the end with wire cutters. Even though this procedure dulls the point, it is still quite serviceable. You can also cover the tip of the needle with tape to prevent the glue from drying out.

This technique is also good to repair old, antique, or recycled frames. Place a bit of glue as deep as possible into the seam between the two sides of the frame. Then put a corner clamp of some type on the corner, and allow it to dry. You can even inject a bit of glue into a nail hole if the nail is loose. Tap the nail again, and let it dry before continuing.

If you can find molding that has a finish on it before you miter the corners, this will greatly simplify the frame-construction process. Just cut the sides of the frame, secure them with clamps, and join them using nails and glue. Building centers sell wood-tone fillers that you can use to fill the nail holes. This final step gives the frame a professional look.

You can also use small corner clamps to grip the molding after gluing. They join the two parts of one corner at a time.

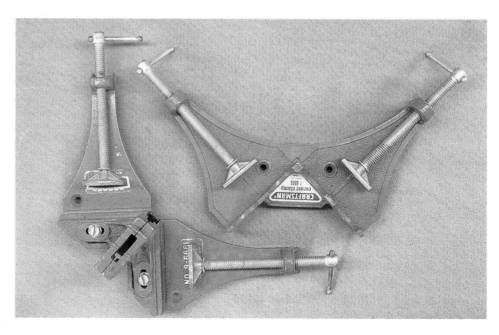

A Merle clamp is ideal for joining all four sides of the frame at one time.

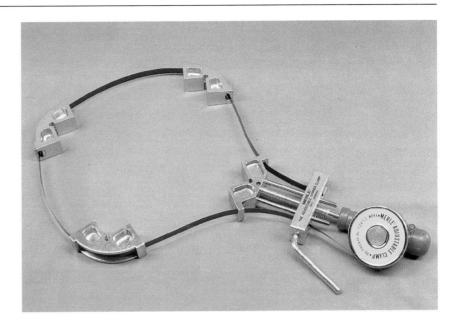

Here, a Merle clamp in action, holding the frame.

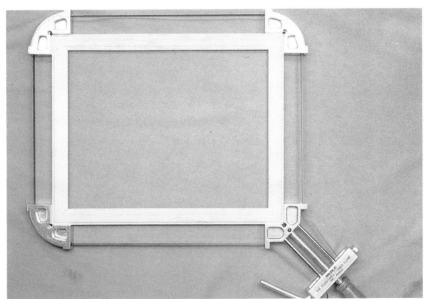

Nail the frame at each corner for insurance. Be careful not to pop the glue loose.

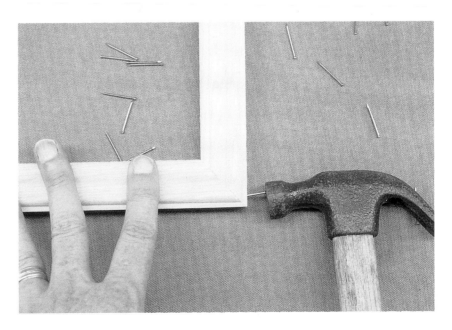

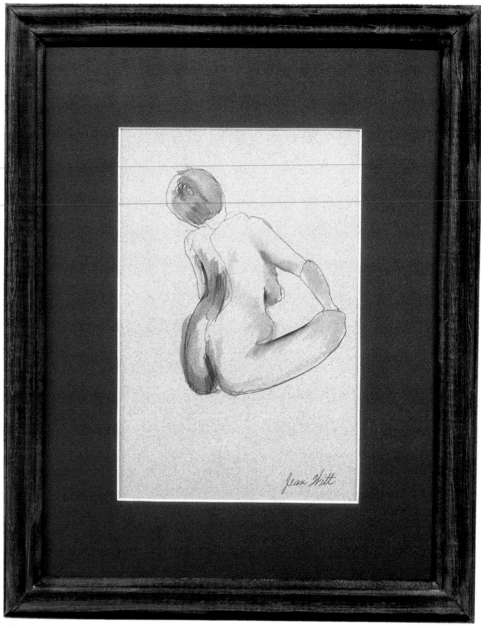

"Lotus." Jean Witt. Aqua media on pastel paper. The frame that sets off this original drawing was mitered in a saw, joined in a Merle clamp, and painted with a dark base coat and aqua antiquing.

MAKING ELABORATE WOODEN FRAMES

When you exhaust all readily available sources for moldings in your frame-making, you might want to consider going to a wholesaler. Many frame-molding wholesalers will deal directly with artists and designers if they're established as a small business. This usually means that they've met some minimal legal requirements and paid a few fees to establish their business name and bank account. Keep in mind, though, that the wholesaler has many storefront clients to protect and might be reluctant to sell to you for two reasons. First, you represent competition to those clients. Second, your volume will be too low. If you encounter resistance, look elsewhere. Some wholesaler will be happy to sell you a few sticks of molding every once in a while. Not all wholesalers deal with only large-scale buyers.

To accurately order or buy sticks of molding, you must calculate the amount by measuring the circumference of the frame. Next, multiply the width of the molding by 8, and add this figure to the circumference of the frame. This is the amount of waste you'll have cutting miters at each corner. Allow an additional 2 inches in length for insurance. Often, wholesalers will give you a chart, so you won't have to do this calculation every time you order.

When you find your sources, a whole new world of molding will open to you. All the lavish, colorful, textured, and elegant moldings the custom shops offer can be yours. You might want to invest in some more specialized equipment when your volume increases to warrant such purchases. A more expensive miter saw, perhaps even a power model, and heavy-duty corner vises could be smart purchases at this point. They are a bit costly but quite precise. With corner vises, you can glue and nail without obstruction. Framing wholesalers usually stock these items, as do catalog framing suppliers.

A few additional tips can come in handy. Moldings that are shipped to you often encounter blows that cause surface damage. You can remove small dents in moldings via a simple method. It isn't always necessary to cut around the dent or ding. Lay the stick of molding on your work surface with the dent upright. Apply distilled water, one drop at a time, with a cotton swab. The wood will most likely absorb the water, allowing the dent to swell and regain its proper profile. You might need to make a couple of attempts, so as the water dries, dab on more, one drop at a time. Only if this method doesn't work should you use steam to help remove a dent. Steam often damages wood finishes and dulls gold-leaf accents, adversely affecting a much larger area than the original dent.

To eliminate a small dent, apply distilled water to it using a cotton swab.

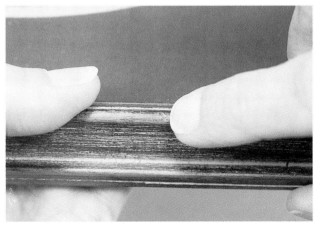

After several applications of distilled water, the dent has swollen back to its original shape, with minor surface damage.

MAKING ELABORATE WOODEN FRAMES

While many artists like the look of distressed or primitive finishes on the frames they use for their artwork, unintentional scrapes and scratches spoil the look of most furniture-finished moldings. These imperfections might have been in the wood originally, or might be the result of improper packaging or rough handling during shipping. You can lessen their visibility with water-based stains or wood-toned graphic markers. Buying one light and one medium stain will enable you to repair scratches on a great number of molding colors. You don't need to have a stain for every color of wood.

Always do a color test first to make sure that the repair will be acceptable. Thin the stain, apply it with a tiny brush, and then immediately rub it off with a soft cloth. Repeat if necessary. Be careful not to put too much stain on the area around the scratch in your attempt to repair it.

The use of graphic markers in wood-toned colors is a fast way to repair scratches and to cover raw wood that is visible at the corners. Once again, the area around the scratch may accept too much of the marker color and look too obvious, so you should do a test. Apply the color in a test area to see how quickly the stain penetrates. Then apply the stain to the scratch, and immediately rub it off with a cloth. Repeat if necessary.

Matching any paints to gold-leaf frames is quite difficult. Some Rub 'n Buff colors work well to repair gold-leaf damage. Rub 'n Buff is a waxy material sold in tubes. Simply rub it on, and then buff it off with a clean cloth. Super-hot gold will need a spot of gold leaf to repair damage. Apply a bit of glue with a toothpick tip, and set a tiny speck of gold leaf on the glue. After you lightly press the gold leaf on the molding with a clean brush, allow it to dry. Brush away any excess gold leaf.

Coloring the cut surface of a mitered corner with graphic markers can dramatically decrease the visibility of the join. Use a wood-toned marker that closely resembles the wood finish of the frame. Apply the marker color along the cut edge of the miter right next to the colored surface. Then when you join the corners, the coloration of the miter helps camouflage the cuts at the corner so they barely show.

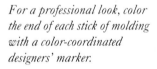
For a professional look, color the end of each stick of molding with a color-coordinated designers' marker.

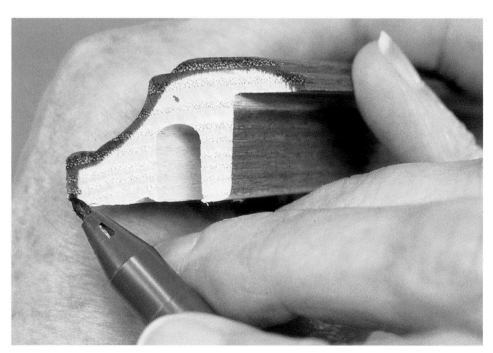

Wide frames on artworks can give them an important look. This ornate, warm copper, wooden frame is compatible and effective with the black of the etching and the single mat.

Untitled. Helgy White. Oil on canvas. This simple, warm gold frame makes the artwork glow. The molding supports rather than competes with the image.

ASSEMBLY AND FITTING

Assembly and fitting are the last steps you must complete when you do any framing project. Naturally, gathering, or assembling, the various components comes first. You must then prepare them. This usually includes cleaning the glass, checking the matting for any scrapes or soil marks, cutting the backing material to size, cutting a paper dust cover, and checking the frame for any necessary touch-ups. For example, filling nail holes with putty that matches the color of the frame are professional touches that make your presentation the best it can be.

After you assemble the parts in their correct order, you can begin the fitting phase. Fitting is the actual joining of the artwork sandwich and the frame into a concise unit, complete and ready to be hung on a wall.

"Windmill." William Thompson. Black-and-white, selenium-toned photograph. The wide borders call attention to the isolation in this picture. The white of the mat matches the whites in the image. The clean simplicity of the silver frame makes it such an integral part of the artwork presentation that it almost becomes invisible.

WOODEN FRAMES

Now that you've gathered a stack of items to put into a frame, you need to think about ways to finish assembling the package. You can go about fitting all the components into the frame several ways. If you're completing a conservation frame job, you must remember to coat the rabbet of the frame with a sealer. The seal protects the artwork from damage produced by contact with wood resins in the frame. Seal the frame with at least two coats of an acrylic-polymer, matte-finish medium, or any other appropriate sealer.

One of the most common methods involves putting each component into the frame individually. First, lay the frame face down on your work surface. Carefully place the cleaned glazing material into the frame. Then in succession, put the mat, mounted art piece, backing, and frame fill-in into the frame. Use a point driver, a brad pusher, or long, thin nails to hold the work in the frame. Attaching a dust cover and hanging wire completes the process.

Initially, this might seem like a great approach. However, debris can easily get in under the glass and ruin the finished look. And there is nothing more exasperating than to complete a project and then find a piece of lint or some other unwanted speck trapped under the glass.

If you modify this closure process just a little, you can significantly reduce the possibility of such a disappointment. Rather than place each item into the frame separately, you can stack and treat the components as a single unit. This sandwich method might seem clumsy at first, but the amount of both time and energy you'll save is considerable.

Place the backing material on the work surface. On top of the backing, set the mounted artwork and the mats that you've cut. Clean only one side of the glass, and immediately turn it over on top of the stack. If time lapses between the cleaning of the glass and its placement on the clean mat and art, reinspect the two. Lint and other debris seem to come from nowhere. Next, clean the top side of the glass. Set the frame over the sandwich, and inspect it a final time for lint.

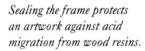

Sealing the frame protects an artwork against acid migration from wood resins.

Next, to affix the sandwich in the frame, turn over this new unit, including the frame, and close it with a point driver, a brad pusher, or long nails. This method of closing eliminates the many opportunities for particles getting into and ruining the look of the framed artwork. Finally, affix a dust cover and hardware. The job is complete.

POINT DRIVERS

Although it is possible to frame a piece of art without a point driver, you won't want to. This tool saves the most time during the assembly and fitting of wooden frames. A point driver shoots a small, flat metal bar into the frame. This bar, in turn, penetrates the wood of the frame to hold the package together firmly. You can easily remove the bars with pliers. Point drivers cost about $75, and the points cost about $20 for a box of 3,000, which is a lifetime supply.

If you can operate a staple gun, you can use a point driver. When you draw the grip handle up toward your palm, a point is driven into the frame. Nothing could be easier. Point drivers work well on wood of any hardness.

Because the point is spring-loaded and driven into the frame with a quick jolt, it is wise to push the frame up against some sort of block in order to brace it. You can utilize, for example, a wall next to your work surface or a 2 × 4 board nailed to your worktable. Without this stationary object, the pressure of the point might pop the frame corner loose. You can remove points when necessary with needle-nose pliers or the tip of wire cutters.

The first step in the fitting process is to place the glass in the frame.

Drop in the mats, with elevation strips in position if necessary.

Place the artwork on mats, and then add the backing.

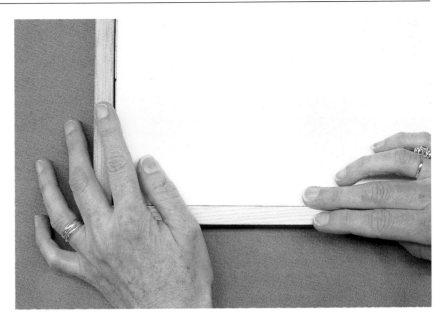

Position the frame over the entire package, turn the assembly over, and close it.

A point driver pushes flat, metal bars into the frame to hold the artwork package in place.

WOODEN FRAMES

BRAD PUSHERS

These hollow-tipped hand tools are inexpensive and simple to use. As its name suggests, a brad pusher enables you to push brads into the frame to hold the artwork package in place. This piece of equipment works well on any soft-to-medium wood. Hard woods, such as oak, are quite difficult to push into. Because the resulting orifice is a bit large, you must hold the nail in position at the tip of the brad pusher. Once you begin the push, the nail is set. Pull back on the band to expose more of the brad. Pushing the brads into the frame takes some strength. One-inch brads pushed in half their length are recommended.

The orifice on the tip of the brad pusher holds the brad while you push it into position.

Here, you see the brad pusher in action.

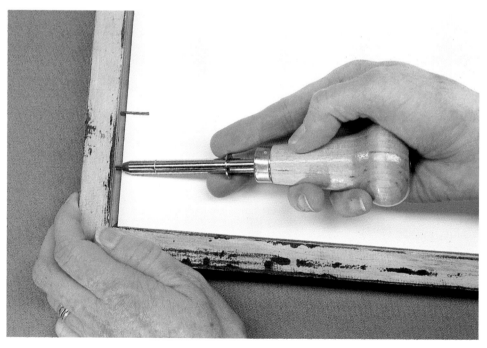

DUST COVERS

Dust covers are used only on wooden frames. They serve several functions, all of which are important to the quality of presentation. Dust covers protect artwork from the back side, preventing dust penetration and accumulation. Dust covers also serve to give a finished look to a wooden-frame project. Without a dust cover, the job isn't complete.

Using two dust covers provides an extra moisture barrier in high-humidity display areas. Simply put the first dust cover on the frame, and then put another cover over the first. For even more protection from humidity penetration, seal the fitted artwork with special frame-sealing tape before attaching the dust covers. Use double-sided tape to hold the dust cover on the frame. This technique is quick and clean and holds well.

The next step is to trim the dust cover; you can use any type of cutting tool for this. Crease the overhang of the backing paper along the edges of the frame. When they're clearly defined, cut along approximately 1/8 inch inside the edges of the frame. You might find it easiest to use a metal-edged ruler and a snap-blade knife or an X-Acto knife. You don't have to push hard on the cutting tool. Remember, the frame's edges are quite close to where you're cutting, and you want to be careful not to damage them. After you remove the excess backing paper, attach the hardware.

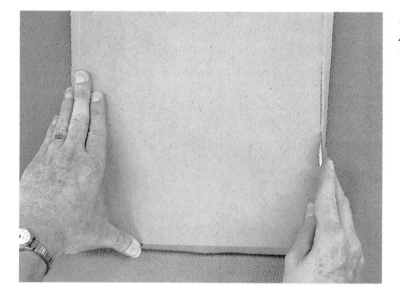

Dust covers help protect the backside of the artwork.

Trim away the excess covering material for a clean, professional presentation.

WOODEN FRAMES

HANGING HARDWARE

You can hang wooden frames with one of two types of hardware. People have used screw eyes for decades to hold the hanging wire. Screw eyes are screw-in shafts with loops at the top. The shaft screws into the wood of the frame, leaving the loop exposed. You string the hanging wire through the loops across the back of the frame.

You might, however, want to try strap hangers (sometimes called mirror hangers) instead. They lay flat against the frame and don't mar the wall during the hanging process. They require separate screws for attachment, so you should have a few short wood screws on hand. You can order these when you buy the strap hangers. Either kind of hanging device is acceptable.

When attaching the wire to the screw eyes or strap hangers, you should make a double pass through the eye of the hanging device. This provides extra holding power and strength. Don't pull the wire between the two hanging devices snug. You should leave enough space for your flattened fist to pass between the back of the dust cover and the wire.

The up-and-down stress that comes from hanging art is unavoidable. But pulling the wire too tightly produces an additional stress on the finished work. When combined with up-and-down stress, this side-to-side stress can break the hanging wire, even when the wire is heavier than required for the weight of the picture. Wrap the tails closely on the hanging wire as soon as you make the double pass through the wire hole.

Screw eyes are one of two types of wire-hanging devices commonly used.

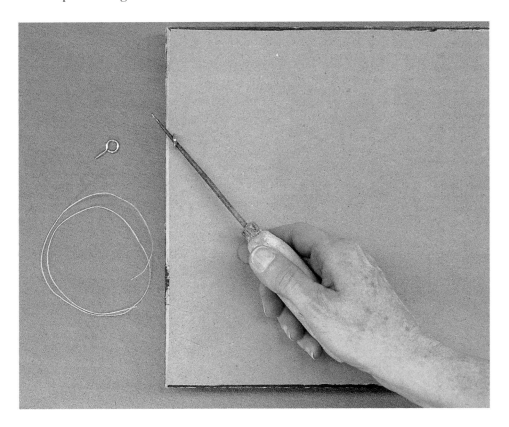

Strap hangers require separate screws to hold them in place.

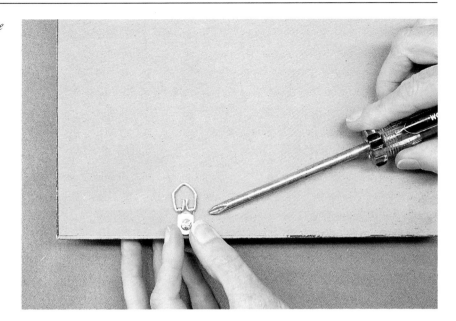

Loop the wire through any wire hanger for added security.

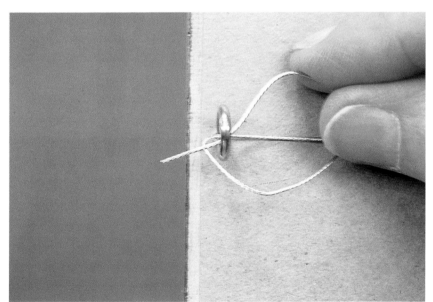

Pull the excess evenly from side to side.

WOODEN FRAMES

The placement of the wire is also important. Current viewing trends suggest that most people prefer having their artworks hug the wall when on display. If you position the wire approximately ⅓ of the distance between the top and bottom of your work, the framed art will hang close to the wall. Positioning the wire too close to the top of the work will permit the wire to show when you hang the piece. And positioning the wire too close to the center will cause the artwork to swing away from the wall when it is displayed. Although some old-fashioned photographs and antique pieces, such as mirrors, might look best hung away from the wall, most artwork looks best as flat as possible.

Measure ⅓ of the way down from the top of the frame, and attach the wire at that spot.

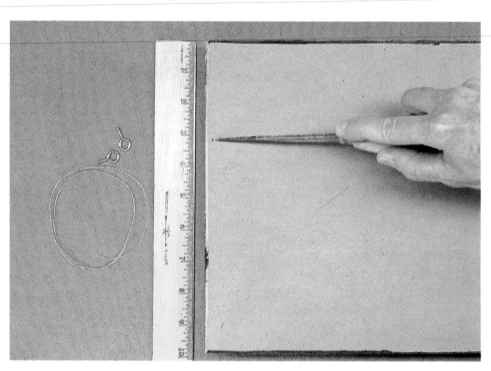

Check to be sure that the wire is positioned in such a way that prevents the wall hanger from showing.

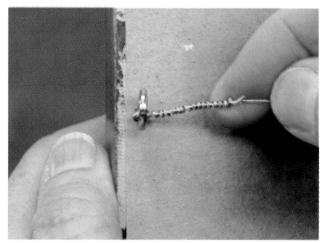

Twist the wire tightly.

"Gulf Coast Lighthouse." Willis Cole, Jr. Watercolor. Watercolor is a medium that lends itself to the rich, warm tones of wooden molding. This softly rounded frame echoes the shape of the lighthouse.

STRETCHED CANVASSES

Framing a stretched canvas is easy and quick, and it doesn't require either glass or backing material. One approach, which people have used for years, attaches the canvas to the frame via long, thin nails. Here, you drive in the nails at an angle, so that the nail catches the edge of the stretcher bar and then continues on into the frame. Make sure that you don't use an angle that is too upright. This could drive the nail not only through the canvas front, but also through the lip of the frame. If this occurs, the frame will usually be damaged beyond repair, so you'll have to make a new frame or buy another one. In addition, the canvas will be severely damaged. Keep in mind that the white pine wood used to make stretcher bars is soft and easy to nail into. You shouldn't have any difficulty.

An alternative method, which calls for canvas clips, is so safe and easy that artists everywhere prefer it to the technique described above. And because the art isn't altered during the process, this is the most artwork-friendly way to join a canvas and a frame. Canvas clips are available at many art-supply stores and framing supply centers. These metal brackets hold the canvas by the stretcher bar tightly and grip the lip of the frame at the same time. You can readily remove them, so changing paintings is quite simple. Canvas clips usually come four to a box and cost about $1.

When framing an oil on canvas, you should consider the protection of a dust cover just as important as it is for any other artwork. Because the canvas needs to breathe, you should provide a breathing space in the dust cover. Design a small, 2 × 3-inch template from scrap mat board to use as a cutting guide. This template can be any shape, but rectangles are customary. Lay the template on the back of the finished dust cover. Cutting out this window enables air to flow into and out of the canvas area.

To protect the art from insect infestation, cover the window with mesh screening. Use frame-sealing tape to hold a small piece of screening over the hole. If you tape the screening over the opening before you attach the cover to the frame, you can position the window low on the backside of the frame. This is the desired placement and finished look.

Oldtime framers have used nails to hold canvasses in frames for years.

Quick and safe to use, canvas clips are the modern method of canvas installation. In addition, you can change them easily.

In order for an oil painting
to breathe, you must cut
a window in the dust cover.
Here, a template of mat
board is used to keep the
shape of the window even.

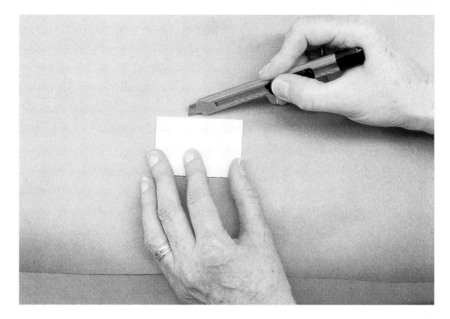

Cover the window with
screening to prevent insect
infestation.

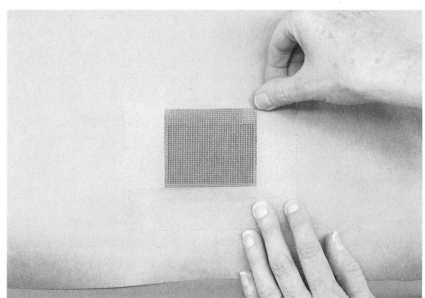

Position the screen-covered
window in the lower center
of the backside of the frame.

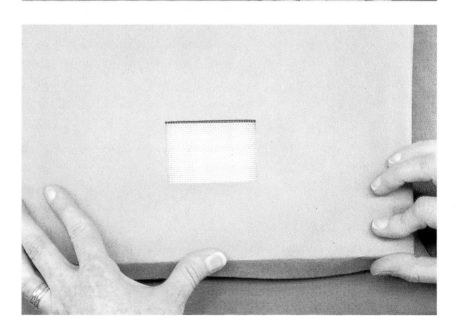

I used a flat-faced, black frame to continue the linear quality of this acrylic on canvas, which I titled "5 Lines and 13 Dots." The edges of the frame become a part of the overall feel of the work.

METAL-FRAME FITTING

For the most part, you automatically learn how to close a metal frame when you actually build the frame. You can't complete the framing without having the artwork sandwich in the frame. But the following tips about metal-frame fitting might interest you.

Because metal frames aren't glued, their corners are basically pushed together and held in place with the hardware on their backside. Because there is no true seal at the corners, metal frames don't protect artwork from humidity as well as wooden frames. Fortunately, however, you can minimize, to some degree, the infiltration of moisture two ways.

In one approach, you seal the backside of the completely framed piece with frame-sealing tape or some other acid-free tape. Position the spring clips first, and then put on the hanging wire. Seal around the edge with the tape. This greatly reduces the amount of humidity that can creep into the frame.

Another method is to put acid-free tape all around the art sandwich before you slide it into the frame. This effectively seals the work in a cocoon. And when you follow this step with putting frame-sealing tape on the backside of the frame, you produce a formidable moisture barrier.

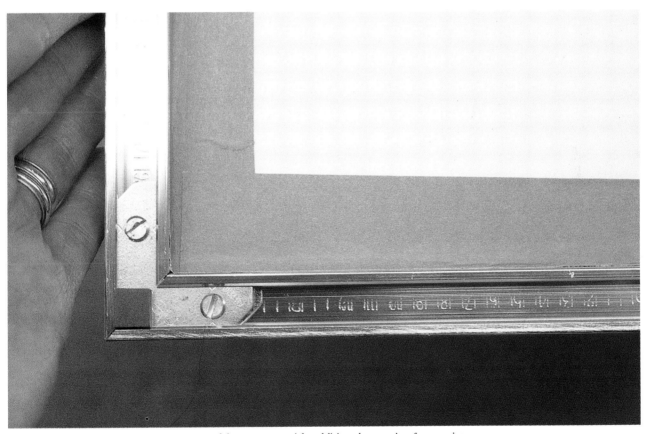

You can use frame-sealing tape on even metal frames to provide additional protection from moisture.

"Shirley Anderson." William Thompson. Black-and-white, selenium-toned photograph. Matting small artworks like this one with extra-wide borders, especially lower borders, can increase their impact. They become true eye-catchers.

SPECIAL FITTING CONSIDERATIONS

By of the nature of large and/or heavy artworks, you must carefully plan—and execute—them from the start. Poor support choices could compromise any stage of their completion. A frame substantial enough to support the work is the basis of a safe presentation.

"Lawson Light." Kathy Earthrowl. Oil on panel. The richness of this painting is due largely to the ties between the golden grasses in the image and the soft gold of the frame. This artwork has an elegant, professional look.

SPECIAL FITTING CONSIDERATIONS

LARGE OR HEAVY ARTWORK

You must pay special attention to two important areas of fitting when you work with large and/or heavy works of art in frames. First, you have to consider the hardware. You must attach it in a way that prevents it from pulling out of wood frames. You can solve this problem in one of two ways. In the first technique, the most important aspect of the attachment is either the length of the screw threads holding the screw eyes or the length of the screw affixing the strap hangers. Use the longest threaded screw eye or screw possible for the frame you're attaching the hardware to.

With large metal frames, flexing can cause severe problems via the displacement of the glazing material. If a large, metal frame flexes enough, it can literally pop the glazing out of the frame lip. To prevent this, use a top-to-bottom tension wire. In the center of the top as well as in the center of the bottom, add a wire holder. Pull a length of wire tautly between the two holders, leaving a tiny amount of flex. This will help align the top and bottom sections of the metal molding even if the sides of the frame flex during transport or hanging.

The second way to help ensure the holding power of the hardware is to use two sets of wire hardware. You can fit two sets of wire holders onto metal moldings. Space them about 1 inch apart, one above the other. Put on the top wire as you would on any framing job, double-looped at the wire hole, and leave the necessary amount of slack. Then put a second wire on the lower set of screw eyes or strap hangers. Begin by attaching it to one of the wire loops, passed twice through the wire hole. Holding the top wire in place and stretched into hanging position, loosely wrap the lower wire around the top wire.

You need to make at least four or five wraps along the length of the top wire. Then gently pull the lower wire to check that you've taken up any slack. While holding the top wire and the second wire with tension, enter and double-wrap the lower wire on the lower piece of hardware at the wire hole. Proceed as usual with the twists of extra tail on the wires.

The third area of major concern involves making sure that the hanger will hold the art piece on the wall. Decorators use and professional framers suggest the use of two wall hooks, the type with a hook at the bottom and an angled nail that goes through a bend at the top of the hanger. Verify that the hooks are designed to hold an object that weighs twice as much as the piece of art you plan to hang. Using a level, place the hooks in the wall horizontally about 6 to 8 inches apart. This provides extra support and keeps the picture level on the wall.

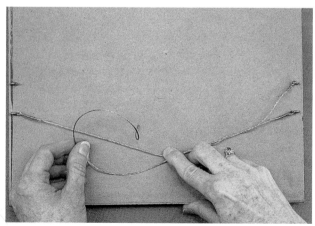

Heavy artworks demand special hanging considerations. Here, a double hanging wire is installed.

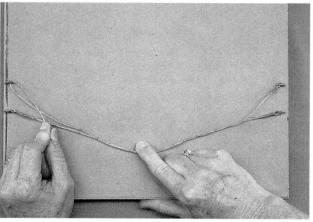

Wrap the second wire around the first. Then even out the tension by eliminating the slack in the second wire.

"The Garden." Helgy White. Oil on canvas. Because this piece of art is so large, special wire-hanging methods were employed to ensure that the hold on the wall was sufficient. Double wires and strap hangers properly supported this oversized painting.

SPECIAL FITTING CONSIDERATIONS

PACKING AND SHIPPING ARTWORK

You need to give some thought to various details when attempting to pack and ship a framed artwork. If at all possible, ship the work without breakable glazing. Broken glass can destroy a piece of art in seconds. Because of the likelihood of blows and drops, you should use much more protective covering than you would otherwise. In fact, when you think you've put on enough padding, put on more. Ideally, a shipping crate should surround the padded and cardboard-covered, framed artwork. When this isn't possible or when the piece of art is fairly small, excessive wrapping is the next best option.

Also, when removing the glass isn't feasible, carefully packaging is the next best line of defense. A triple layer of bubble wrap placed immediately around the artwork is the first of several steps in wrapping. After securing these layers of bubble wrap, construct an oversized covering of corrugated cardboard and secure it well with strapping tape or some other strong tape. Wrap this bundle in two or three additional layers of bubble wrap. Construct another corrugated "envelope," and tape well around its edges. After you put a final two to three layers of bubble wrap around the artwork and follow this with a box all around the piece, the artwork will be ready for shipping.

To prepare glazed art pieces for transport during a household move, wrap three layers of bubble wrap around them. Secure the artwork with tape, and then stand them upright in a carton or crate. In this way, you can transport pieces of art vertically, several to a box. Be aware, however, that this isn't suitable for long-term or common-carrier shipping. Casual wrapping like this is appropriate only for hand packing, hand transporting, and hand delivery.

PACKAGING ARTWORK FOR EXHIBITION

When you ship artworks for display in a public exhibition, you should think about the entire process from start to finish. For the exhibition itself, you should protect the work with glazing. More and more show organizers are specifying Plexiglas or some other acrylic sheeting for exhibited work. Plexiglas is difficult to break, so you have less worry about damage during shipping, during the show, and during the return trip.

Throughout this entire time, the safety of your artwork should be paramount. You not only want it to arrive intact, but to be wrapped in such a way that the packaging can be used to securely wrap and return the work to you. A crate is the best possible shipping method. Finally, because you aren't in control of the rewrapping of your artwork, giving the exhibition staff every possible assistance is recommended. You might want to include packing instructions for the return trip or extra padding as a precaution.

Shipping glazed artwork, such as this 5 × 6-inch framed piece, necessitates ample wrapping and padding.

With just a single layer of bubble wrap, the size of the artwork increases to more than 6 × 7 inches.

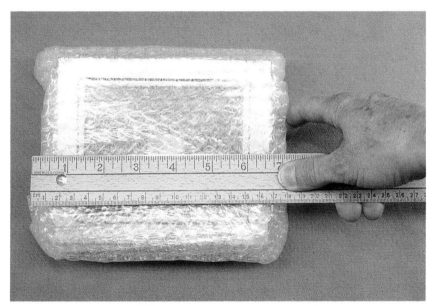

The first of two cardboard coverings increases the size to 12 × 16 inches. Correctly padded, the piece should measure at least 20 × 24 inches to provide adequate protection. The entire bundle should then be put into a large box with additional padding.

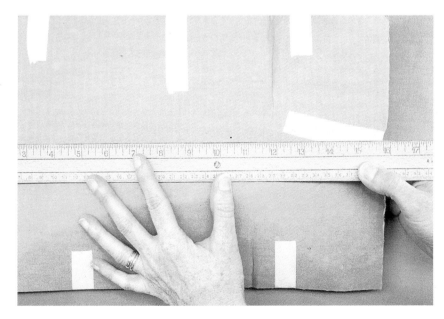

GLOSSARY

Acid-free—A blanket term used to describe any material that doesn't contain acid. This can be a product that is naturally acid-free, such as rag matting, or one whose acidity has been neutralized with calcium.

All-rag mat board—A matting material that contains only cotton rag fibers and has a white core.

Archival—A term used to describe a completely acid-free presentation, mounting, or product.

Artists' tape—An acid-free paper tape with a neutral pH adhesive. The tape has many framing uses, such as serving as a hinging material.

Barrier paper—An all-rag paper that helps to isolate an artwork from contact with acid-bearing materials.

Beveled edge—A perfect, 45-degree, angular cut. It exposes 1/16 inch of core color all around the mat window.

Black-core mats—These dramatic mats have black cores and a limited range of surface colors.

Colored core mats—These mats have a limited variety of core colors: blue, pink, green, brown, and maroon.

Conservation mounting—Mounting that protects an artwork from any contact with acid. Completed with all-rag, acid-free materials.

Corner hardware—The brackets that hold the corners of metal moldings together.

Corner clamps and vises—Devices used to join mitered sticks of molding, one corner at a time.

Couching—A crisscross stitchery pattern used to hold the excess fabric of a mounted stitchery. Pronounced kooching.

Custom framing—Framing done by a professional in a shop dedicated to that work.

Deckle—The decorative, uneven, handmade look on the edges of fine-quality papers.

Double-sided tape—A special tape used to attach paper to paper, mats to mats, dust covers to frames, foamboard to foamboard, and similar joins. The tape's sticky surface is dispensed on a silicone paper backing that is placed, pressed, and then peeled to reveal the sticky strip.

Dry-sheet adhesives—Acid-free adhesives in film or droplet-style sheet form that are transferred to the backside of an artwork for easy mounting onto a suitable backing.

Dust cover—A protective paper covering on the back of wooden frames.

Elevation—Raising mats and artwork by inserting strips of foamboard.

Filmoplast—An acid-free paper tape with PVA adhesive (neutral pH).

Fitting—The closure and finishing of a frame.

Fixative—A spray product used to hold fine-powder art materials on the surface of a drawing or painting.

Flange—A commercially made acetate strip attached to an all-rag base. The acetate extends over the edge of the artwork. The base is coated with an acid-free adhesive that holds the flange in place.

Floated artwork—A piece of art suspended on a colored field and hinged into place with V or S hinges. The artwork can be elevated for a special sense of dimension.

Foamboard—The professionals' choice of a backing and support material. Lightweight, rigid, easy to cut, clean, and white, it has a very low acid content, a clay-coated top, and bottom papers with a rigid foam center.

Frame-sealing tape—Specially designed for the framing industry, this acid-free tape is used to seal the backs of frames.

Frame size—The measurement that equals the image size plus all mat border widths.

Glazing—Glass and glass-type materials that cover a framed artwork.

Gummed linen tape—Linen tape coated with a natural adhesive that must be moistened for activation. Can be reversed and removed with pure water.

Hinges—Strips of linen tape, or rice paper and rice starch. Can be folded and reinforced to hold an artwork in place with as little contact as possible. Considered acid-free and/or conservation-mounting materials depending on the method used.

Hook—A curve that occurs in the corner of a mat window. The primary cause is a dull blade.

Image size—The actual picture area of a piece of art, excluding all borders.

Limited-edition artwork—Duplicates of an original artwork. Prints that are created one at a time even though pulled from the same master are considered limited editions when signed and numbered accordingly. Photographic lithographs that are signed and numbered are also limited editions.

Linen tape—A pure linen tape coated with an all-natural adhesive. Ideal for hinges.

Miter box—A device to aid in the sawing of molding into various angles. Used with a miter saw.

Moisture barrier—Any material used to prevent the entry of moisture into a framed artwork.

Museum mat board—Four thin layers of all-rag material bonded with an all-natural adhesive. White or cream in color throughout.

Neutral pH—A pH of 7. Neither acid nor alkaline.

Original artwork—A one-of-a-kind art creation that is executed from an original idea.

Overcuts—Cuts that extend slightly past the corners of a mat window.

Photo-mounting corners—Special acid-free corners reminiscent of old scrapbook corners. Sticky-backed, they attach quickly and easily.

Point driver—A handheld, spring-loaded fitting device. Drives in a flat metal bar that holds artwork in a wooded frame.

Prop—Additional support used along the lower edge of a large, heavy piece of art during a conservation mounting. Butted against the base of the artwork and held with acid-free tape.

Rabbet—The channel cut into a wooded frame into which the artwork sandwich is placed.

Ready-made frames—Frames purchased ready to fit with artwork.

Regular mat board—Wood-pulp-base matting buffered with calcium carbonate to a neutral pH. Core has a soft, off-white color.

Rice paper—A special paper used to create hinges. Ordinarily torn to size and attached with rice starch.

Rice starch—A completely natural adhesive. This ancient mounting material is still used today.

Sandwich—The entire artwork package: glass, mat, mounted artwork, and backing.

Score line—The initial scratch on the surface of glass in preparation for cutting glass to size.

S hinge—A two-piece hinge shaped like that letter. Half of the vertical piece of hinge material is attached to the back of an artwork. The other half is passed through a slit in the backing and crossed over on the backside for support. Used to suspend an artwork on a colored field.

Silicone adhesive—A clear, super-bonding adhesive. Ideal for mounting heavy or unusual shapes to background mats.

Sling—A small piece of all-rag paper pleated in the center and used during the conservation mounting of large artworks. One end of a sling is slipped beneath the piece of art, and its fold and remaining tail are on top of the artwork. Acid-free tape holds a sling in place.

Spacer—A lifting strip, usually associated with lifting glass off a piece of art. Either made out of strips of mat board or commercially manufactured out of plastic.

Spray adhesive—An aerosol-spray, high-tack glue. Must be used with caution because inhaling the overspray is dangerous.

Sticky boards—Mounting boards produced for mounting stitchery. Glues used can discolor stitchery over time. They can also damage stitchery unless the adhesive is acid-free. Use with caution.

Surround mat—A mat cut to help hold a thick, somewhat three-dimensional piece of art. This mat holds the artwork between the decorative mats on top of it and the backing.

T hinge—A two-piece hinge configured to resemble that letter. Composed of one vertical piece and at least one horizontal piece.

Table-top mat cutter—A cutter with a base, a fixed cutting bar, and a cutting head.

Thumb nail—A small slot cut in each end of a mitered molding stick. The corners are glued together, and a small plastic wedge is tapped into the slot.

Ultraviolet—The spectrum of light that causes severe damage to artworks.

Undercuts—Cuts that don't extend completely to the corner. Must be hand-cut to finish window removal.

V hinge—A two-piece hinge in which the long vertical piece is folded in half. The part that isn't attached to the artwork is crossed with a support strip.

Wet mounting—A term associated with either spray mounting or brayed-on liquid adhesive.

Window—The opening cut into a mat.

RESOURCES

GENERAL ART AND
FRAMING MATERIALS

Art Express
P.O. Box 216
Columbia, SC 29221
800-535-5908

Artist and Display
9015 West Burleigh
Milwaukee, WI 53222
800-722-7450 (Wisconsin only)
414-442-9100

Art Max
P.O. Box 330
Pacific Grove, CA 93950
800-4ARTMAX

Coop Artists' Materials
P.O. Box 53097
Atlanta, GA 30355
800-877-3242

Dick Blick Art Materials
P.O. Box 1267
Galesburg, IL 61401
800-447-8192

Dixie Art Supply
2512 Jefferson Highway
New Orleans, LA 70121
800-783-2612

Herwick's Art Supply
301 Broadway
San Antonio, TX 78205
210-227-1349

Hickory Knoll Studio (ClearGroovers)
1421 Walnut Lane
Kingwood, TX 77339
713-358-3060

Jerry's Artarama
P.O. Box 1105
New Hyde Park, NY 11040
800-U-Artist

Light Impressions
P.O. Box 940
Rochester, NY 14603
800-828-6216

Texas Art Supply
2001 Montrose Boulevard
Houston, TX 77006
800-888-9278

FRAMES AND FRAMING
SUPPLIES

American Frame Corporation
400 Tomahawk Drive
Maumee, OH 43537
800-322-5899

Frame Fit Company
P.O. Box 8926
Philadelphia, PA 19135
800-523-3693

Frame Wealth
R.D. 2, Box 261-7
Ortego, NY 13825
800-524-8582

Franken Frames
609 West Walnut
Johnson City, TN 37604
800-322-5899

Graphic Dimensions, Ltd.
2103 Brentwood Street
High Point, NC 27263
800-221-0262

M & M Distributors
Route 522
P.O. Box 189
Tennent, NJ 07768
800-526-2302

The Mettle Company
P.O. Box 525
Fanwood, NJ 07023
800-621-1329

United Manufacturers Supply, Inc.
80 Gordon Drive
Syosset, NY 11791
800-645-7260

HANDS-ON FRAMING
WORKSHOPS

Janean S. Thompson
Certified Picture Framer
1421 Walnut Lane
Kingwood, TX 77339
713-358-3060

Total At Home Picture Framing
P.O. Box 626
Island Lake, IL 60042
708-526-0030

INDEX

INDEX